A Writer's Guide to Getting Published in Magazines

JJ DeSpain

A Writer's Guide to Getting Published in Magazines

JJ DeSpain

ALETHEIA
Publications

WITHDRAWN

DeSpain, JJ
A Writer's Guide to Getting Published in Magazines

Library of Congress Catalog Card Number: 99-97215
ISBN: 1-929129-01-7

Cover design: Bart Solenthaler
Copyeditor: David R. Hall
Interior design and composition: Guy J. Smith

Aletheia Publications, Inc.
46 Bell Hollow Rd.
Putnam Valley, NY 10579

Printed in Canada
10 9 8 7 6 5 4 3 2 1

Contents

Acknowledgments

Joel Despain—My husband, reader, truest supporter, and constant source of encouragement

Patricia Irwin—My reader, and my trusted and literate friend

The Midwest Writers Workshop (Muncie, Indiana)—The place where I learned I could be a writer

My magazine editors, good and bad—You have taught me well

Introduction

*Writing is like religion. Every man who feels the call
must work out his own salvation.*
                    —George Horace Lorimer

GEORGE HORACE LORIMER was a newspaper reporter who took
over as editor of a failing magazine in 1897 and turned it into
one of the biggest magazine success stories this country has
ever seen. That magazine, the *Saturday Evening Post,* was
founded in 1821 and is still published today. While it has un-
dergone changes, including a period when publication ceased,
it stands as a tribute to a body of writing that was neither
welcomed nor easily established in the United States but has
fought its way into recognition, wide acceptance, and the
homes of many Americans.

During this country's early days, the purpose of books
was to establish the written law and discuss the newly emerg-
ing religious and political freedoms. Newspapers found a place
in cities that were too large for the traditional word of mouth
communication to work. But magazines were unnecessary,
so they didn't come onto the scene until 1741, 100 years after

the publication of America's first book, *The Bay Psalm Book,* and 50 years after the first American newspaper, *Publick Occurrence Both Foreign and Domestick,* hit the streets. There was opposition to the magazine form. It represented the best of British society, and in a country struggling to find its own identity the British standard was not accepted. Also, magazines were read only by the upper class, a very small segment of the population, making publication for so few people financially impractical.

In 1740 Benjamin Franklin conceived the idea of the first American magazine: *The General Magazine and Historical Chronicle, for All the British Plantations in America.* Even so, Andrew Bradford takes his place in history for publishing the first American magazine, *The American Magazine, or A Monthly View of the Political State of the British Colonies,* in 1741, three days before the release of Franklin's first issue. Neither was successful. A postal law was enacted, making the delivery of magazines a matter of a postmaster's choice, not law. Postal rates for magazines were high, too, making the cost of magazine delivery a hardship. Franklin found a way around that problem, however. Both his and Bradford's magazines were published in Philadelphia, and because Franklin was Philadelphia's postmaster at the time, he waived all postal fees for his own magazine. But even that advantage wasn't enough to keep his magazine afloat for long.

At that time magazines were difficult to produce. Fifteenth-century hand presses were still used, turning out one page at a time. Paper and ink had to be imported from Britain. America's few businesses could not afford the cost of advertising, which was then, as today, a magazine's primary financial resource. So, with postal difficulties, production problems, and a lack of readers, magazines had a tough time getting off the ground. And when they did get going, most folded within the first year.

The magazine industry kept plugging away, though, thanks to visionaries like Benjamin Franklin, Thomas Paine, and Noah Webster, who saw the potential for a new medium for expression other than that found in books and newspapers. Magazines offered commentary and information on events of the day, and glimpses of politicians and religious leaders, and served as a tour guide of a country yet to be explored, complete with pictures to go with the stories. One of the first magazine engravers was Paul Revere. His counterpart today is the magazine photographer.

Against the odds, American magazines started to edge forward once they had been created, an onward march that has not stopped. Early issues dealt with slavery, woman suffrage, and education. Today's magazine pages include stories about racial injustices, women's issues, and education. In the eighteenth century, magazine readers loved to read about celebrities. When you look at current magazines at the grocery store checkout stand, how many have celebrities on the cover? Things haven't changed all that much. American magazines reflected the concerns of society at their inception, and they still do.

From the humble origins of the American magazine until now, the one consistent factor in every issue ever published is the writer. We are the ones who made magazines succeed in the beginning and are the ones who are still responsible for their success. We write the stories, analyze trends and society standards to find the best way to write our stories, and influence the people who read our work. We always have, even when early articles were read by, at the most, 1600 people. We still do today, when one article can reach millions of people.

When I first started writing magazine articles, it didn't occur to me that magazine writers have influence, that our words are read and digested by seniors who need a better way to find good health care or by teens struggling with the complex issues of peer pressure. People who pick up a magazine are looking for information that they don't already have or for something that can help make their lives better. Providing that is an awesome responsibility.

One of my earliest articles was about Randy Moore, a 17-year-old boy who was severely disabled in an accident. On his way home from a school dance, his car hit an icy patch and in the blink of an eye he went from being a handsome, energetic high school senior full of hopes and dreams to a young man who had to fight for every breath he would draw for the rest of his life. In spite of the overwhelming odds against Randy, he wanted independence and dignity, and he became a crusader for accessible public transportation in his town. He won the battle.

When the story was published, I was pleased with the artwork and layout, and I was happy that it had gone to press unedited. Taking all these elements into consideration, I tagged the work a success.

Three months later I received a letter from a woman in Nigeria. She was counseling a family who were trying to come to terms with their son's accident. The accident was similar to the one I had written about, and their son was close to Randy's age. Judging from the letter, his condition was much like Randy's, too. Somehow this counselor had come across my article. I don't know how it happened, because it was printed in a small-circulation magazine, in English, and should never have made it to Nigeria. But it did, and even with the counselor's very limited understanding of English, she knew this was the story that would make a difference to two parents struggling to figure out how their son could find a new life as a person with a disability.

After I read the counselor's letter and thought about the impact my story had made on a very real family, the way I approached my writing changed. It wasn't about the best artwork anymore, or about getting published unedited. It was about a huge responsibility to my readers. To be honest, until that time I had never considered the reader a part of my article. Today, when I write an article about senior citizen health care, the 70-year-old woman who will read it is in the front of my mind. And when I write an article about peer pressure, the 14-year-old boy who is holding out against the drugs his friends want him to take is the person I think about before I turn on my computer. My words influence these people and make a difference in their lives. While I may never meet the people who take my advice, I know that they are out there, reading and taking to heart the words I write.

It doesn't matter if we call ourselves magazinists, journalists, or magazine writers. We're all in the same boat, or at least we hope to be climbing into that boat soon. The purpose of *A Writer's Guide to Getting Published in Magazines* is to help the climbers understand the process of taking an idea and turning it into something that people will read and trust. Because the goal of most magazine writers is to find the success that generates income, this book deals only with writing for commercial magazines, not with writing for literary or academic journals.

Getting published is never a guaranteed outcome of writing, and this book does not make that guarantee to any writer. Rather, it offers suggestions and information that will help aspiring magazine writers understand the industry and the process of magazine writing. It will also help them find the tools necessary to build a career in which a few words strung into a few sentences can give hope to a heartbroken family in Nigeria.

1

Do You Have What It Takes to Be a Magazine Writer?

Nothing is so hard, but search will find it out.
—Robert Herrick

YOUR LOVE of writing started long before you picked up this book. It was there when you were in grade school, most likely, or high school. You didn't just wake up one morning and proclaim, "Today I'm going to be a writer." You've dreamed about it for years, and truly desired it for almost as long. You've struggled with bits and pieces of sentences and ideas you've committed to paper, trying to organize them into a logical story, and you've read the results of other writers' bits and pieces and thought, "I can do better than that." You have an idea for an article in the forefront of your mind right now, with another trying to push its way to the head of the line.

Before you write, you must first determine where you fit into the scheme of things. *Freelance* (or *free-lance*) is defined as "a writer, actor, etc. who is not under contract for regular work but sells his writings or services to any buyer." This book deals with freelance writing for magazines. Because you have read to this point, magazine writing is probably something you'd like to do. It's a good choice. Magazines provide steady work, there are more freelance articles published every year than books, they exist for every special interest under the sun, and they are approachable by any writer, including the beginner. It takes a writer with some special traits to succeed in the magazines, however. Here are three of them:

- Persistence
- Energy
- Curiosity

Persistence is a magazine writer's constant companion, because a magazine career is not easy to start or maintain. Rejection rates are high, and you're competing with thousands of other writers for the same publishing slot each time you submit a manuscript or a query letter (a letter proposing an article you would like to write). Holding firmly to your purpose in spite of the obstacles is a necessary ingredient in anything you deem publishable, because until you've established a reputation, the magazine publishing industry is not going to roll out a red carpet for you. You'll be rejected over and over again, and persistence will be needed to keep you going back even when the threat of another rejection looms. That persistence will pay off, though. When you keep going back, someone will eventually notice you. After you are noticed, you'll receive a serious look, and finally that serious look will turn into an opportunity to prove yourself. If you are not persistent, if you don't keep going back, no one will notice. And when no one notices, you won't be published.

Energy is also a prerequisite for magazine writing. At the beginning of a career, most writers wisely choose not to pursue writing as their only means of support, because magazine income probably will not support them for some time to come. Until you've launched a solid career, holding on to that proverbial day job is advisable, especially when you recognize that the average income for freelance magazine writers working a minimum of thirty hours a week is slightly less than $5000 per year. This income will rise with time and effort, but until then it takes extra energy to drag yourself to the library after your regular hard day's work to start your second hard day's work. Turning on your computer to begin your second job, long after everyone's in bed and you'd like to be in bed too, can be backbreaking. And even when your magazine writing turns into a full-time occupation, that high energy level will still be necessary to complete the increased number of jobs coming your way.

As you move into full-time writing, don't be surprised to find that the job you hoped would occupy no more than forty hours of your week will consume as much as sixty or seventy. It happens. While part-time magazine writers may have one or two projects going at any given time, full-time writers may have to juggle a dozen or more. That many deadlines staring you in the face at once means that your energy level is as vital to your writing life as food and water are to your physical life.

Curiosity creates ideas, and ideas generate publishable work. Curiosity takes the mundane and turns it into something salable. When you're sitting in your dentist's chair with your mouth open, listening to him ramble on about a patient who drives him crazy, do you merely let his complaints go in one ear and out the other, or do you wonder what other things might irritate the man holding the drill in your mouth? Perhaps there's an article in that thought—"Ten Things That Tick Off Your Dentist." A curious writer takes in everything around him, investigates it further, then considers it in terms of article potential.

Are you persistent, energetic, and curious? Be honest with yourself here, because it takes all three to find success in writing for magazines. Ask yourself if you're emotionally capable of dropping another query into the mail after you've had a succession of sixty straight rejections. Can you conduct a phone interview at three in the morning, if that's the only time your expert in a distant time zone is available? Is there always a bigger picture in everything you see or experience? Answering "no" suggests that magazine writing isn't for you, but that's okay. Magazine freelancing is tough. The work is not consistent, the paychecks can be few and far between, the competition will beat you nine times out of ten, and nothing comes without a fight and far more effort than you thought it would take. To build a career in the magazines, a successful writer must be as tough as the industry in which he is seeking employment, and there's nothing worse than choosing a career path, then planning and working toward it, only to find that you should have been doing something else all along.

Answering "yes"—affirming that you are persistent, energetic, and curious—means that you possess the most important attributes necessary for establishing the career you want. Sure, the drawbacks are still there, but so are the exciting steps forward—the first byline and paycheck, going from a local to a national magazine where millions are reading your words instead of thousands, the chance to become the competition that other writers want to beat. When you can honestly say "yes" to these questions, you are on your way.

Why Do I Want to Write?

Magazine writing is a career choice that has to be driven every step of the way, and you are the only one in the driver's seat. Jobs rarely line up on your doorstep—it's up to you to find, develop, and sell your own projects. There are no benefits: no sick days, no holidays. No work means no pay. And there are never any guarantees that because you have a job this week, you'll have one the next.

"Hard work. Pay not guaranteed. Hours unpredictable. No benefits." Would you respond to such an ad in the classifieds?

Stepping into the role of freelance magazine writer is filled with uncertainty, especially at first, and you should give some thought as to why you want to take that step. Most writers will tell you that despite the hardships it's the greatest career in the world, but what are you telling yourself? I write…

Because it is a burning passion.
Because others have found they can make a living
    doing it.
Because I like to see my name in print.

To be considered an authority on the subject.
To further my career.
To hang on to the career I have.
To teach, or provide a service.
To entertain.
Because I've had incredible life experiences I'd like to
    share.

Any reason is a good one to start a magazine writing career, except, perhaps, writing to become wealthy or famous. Wealth rarely happens in magazine writing. The same holds true for fame. All the other reasons are good. You should keep in mind your own reasons for wanting a magazine career when that career isn't progressing the way you would like.

Make a list of your own top five reasons for writing, then stick it on the side of your computer to remind yourself there's a purpose to the struggle. Here's one form it could take.

Why do I want to be a magazine writer?
1. I love to write.
2. I love to write.
3. I love to write.
4. I love to write.
5. I love to write.

Who said the reasons have to be different? One good reason can make a career.

Education Versus Talent

Most writers are born with a seed of writing talent that grows, then blossoms, at some point in their life. Others work hard to develop their skills along the way. Somehow, though, whether a teacher once said you were a good writer or you took an honest look at something you wrote and decided it was good, you have the gut feeling you are meant to write. So do you need a college degree to get started?

Absolutely not. The requirements for the job are writing talent, skill, and a love of writing. A college degree in a writing discipline is only a bonus, and unlike what happens in most other jobs, in writing, your boss—the editor—will not ask to see that piece of paper certifying your degree. The only piece of paper she wants is the query you sent in, or the finished manuscript. Even so, don't quit in the middle of your journalism class, announcing to your professor that you don't need the education because you already have the talent and a love for the craft. Everything counts toward success, including any education you've received or will receive.

If you lack the education, though, and it is not available to you in the conventional classroom form or you just plain don't want to sit through a writing class, don't worry. Many writing careers have been based on solid skill without that diploma. The craft of good writing can be learned, and your library is probably filled with volumes that teach everything from the basics to the finer details. A persistent writer, even one without a diploma, will find those volumes and study them. He will take notes, pull out the information he needs, then read some more. Eventually, he will add his learning to his talent and come up with the skills necessary for success. In other words, Learning (not necessarily formal education) + Talent = Skill.

How Does My Work Measure Up?

The dictionary defines subjective as "of, affected by, or produced by the mind or a particular state of the mind; of, or resulting from the feelings or temperament of the subject or person thinking; determined by and emphasizing the ideas, thoughts, feelings, etc. of the artist, writer, or speaker." Objective, on the other hand, is "without bias or prejudice; detached; impersonal. Determined by, and emphasizing the feelings and temperament of the object, or thing dealt with, rather than the thoughts, feelings, etc. of the artist, writer, or speaker." Simply put, subjectivity takes a personal look, objectivity an unbiased look.

Evaluating your own writing talent is both a subjective and an objective process. As a subjective writer, you imbue your writing with everything in your repertoire that will make it better. You make your work personal and evaluate it from your personal perspective. As an objective writer, you are an editor. All writers must become editors of their own work. You step away from your personal connection to the piece and look at it impartially as if you hadn't written it. Being both subjective and objective isn't easy, especially when your talent is on the line, but approaching your writing from both viewpoints is necessary in order to gain insight into how your work measures up to work already being published.

How can you determine if your work measures up?

1. Read the writing trade magazines (magazines that cover the news of a specific trade or industry) to see what successful writers are saying about writing. Try *Writer's Digest*, *Byline*, or *The Writer*, or consult *The National Directory of Magazines* or the *Literary Marketplace (LMP)* for more choices, and browse your library's writing resource shelf to find books on the subject.
2. Do an online search for writing resources.
3. Ask other writers what trade magazines and books they recommend.
4. Take a writing course. You don't have to enroll in journalism or creative writing classes at your local university. Instead, consult a university catalog for continuing education classes. They are usually less expensive than regular classes and often do not meet for as long as an entire semester. If your local university does not offer a writing course as part of its continuing education, call and make the request that it do so.
5. Check with your library and local bookstores for writing classes, too. Occasionally, writers promoting new works will present brief classes.
6. Attend a writing seminar. These last anywhere from a few hours to a few days, offering instruction by writers well-established in their careers. Check the *Literary Marketplace, Writer's Market, Writer's Digest,* and a university writing department for upcoming seminars and conferences. Many larger newspapers also sponsor writing seminars.

7. Take advantage of manuscript critiquing services offered through a writing seminar, by one of the seminar instructors. A few dollars may buy you a wealth of information about your writing. Don't waste your money on professional critiquing services, however. They can cost more than what you'll make on your article, and since there are no standards governing critiquing services, you may be evaluated by someone who has less writing experience than you.

8. Join a critique group, or find your writing peers and create one. You may meet them at a writing seminar or in a class you're taking. Advertising on library, bookstore, and university bulletin boards is another good way to locate other writers. Critique groups can be brutal, but they can also provide that key ingredient necessary to transform your manuscript from ho-hum into salable. Don't forget that members of a critique group are in the same boat as you. They are trying to get published too, and they're relying on you to help them achieve their goals, just as you are relying on them.

   One cautionary word on writers' critique groups. Many writers become so heavily invested in their group that they forgo their original goal of trying to produce what an editor wants, opting instead to produce something suitable for their critique group. Keep in mind that a critique group should be a help, not a crutch. It should never become the targeted destination for your work.

9. Corner a professional writer, that being defined as someone who is published regularly and makes a living from it. You'll meet writers at conferences, bookstores, and libraries, at the mall, in the grocery store, and just about anyplace else you go. When you do, ask questions. Don't be bashful. Bend an ear, pick a brain. The worst thing that can happen is you'll be refused, but the best thing is you'll learn something that will help you get published.

Establishing yourself in writing circles is the best way to judge your talent level. You may find it's much better than you expected, or much worse. Either way, you know where you stand, and you can guide your career accordingly. Maybe it's time to send out a query letter. Or maybe you need to go back and read another book and attend a further seminar. Whatever the case, once you connect yourself with the field in which you would like to work, the standards by which you will judge yourself will become more apparent.

The true measure of a writer is found in his burning desire to write something—anything—and he's restless when he's not writing. The true measure of a writer is found in the drive that forces him to learn more than he already knows—to check every available source and ask questions whenever an opportunity presents itself. He is compelled to sit down at the computer to write every time he passes by, and his scheduled two-hour writing session passes so quickly it feels more like twenty minutes. Most of all, the true measure of a writer is found in his efforts to improve his craft, every day. All writers—even those who have spent a lifetime writing—feel, and do, these things. If they don't, their work stagnates, opening a door for an eager new writer who is ready and able to fill their pages.

That new writer just might be you.

Why Choose Magazines?

There are many reasons writers choose magazines over other types of writing. Have you asked yourself why you're reading a book on magazine writing and not on how to sell a romance novel?

The majority of the better-paying magazines publish nonfiction, and most people who read magazines want knowledge and answers in a quick and easy-to-understand format. "How can I get rid of the clutter in my closet?" Why read a 200-page book when you can find the answer in a 2,000-word article?

Wanting to offer solutions is a great reason to be a magazine writer, and in fact most nonfiction articles fall into the advice category. Consider a few other reasons for choosing magazines:

- A magazine article, from conception to end product, will take anywhere from a few hours to several days to research and write. But a book might take months or years, and the idea that a project can be wrapped up in a relatively short period of time is appealing to many writers. Magazine writing is a logical choice for those who want to produce a publishable work, quickly, and get on to the next project.
- In magazine writing you deal with a wide variety of topics instead of committing yourself to one for a matter of months, as in writing a book.
- Many writers use one career as a starting point to launch another, and magazines are a good way to launch a nonfiction career in books.

There is, however, an incorrect notion coming from many writing sources that magazines are the easiest way to start a writing career. The truth is that breaking into magazines is rarely easy, and if you are approaching it only as a means of finding another career, the delay in starting what you really want to do will rob you of precious time in which you could be pursuing your true goal.

There's another prevailing and equally incorrect notion that magazine writing not only is the easiest way to get published but is easy work. An attendee at a writing conference once claimed that she could write, in her sleep, all those "How to Save Money on Your Grocery Shopping" articles she sees in the women's magazines. "Anybody can write that stuff," she said. Writing may be easy for most writers—and it should be—but the entire process of getting published is anything but easy because accompanying your writing skill must be an ability to pitch it to an editor, expertise in negotiating the terms of the contract, plus knowledge of the industry, magazine markets, and editors. Then you've got to determine what was published in the magazine you're approaching prior to your approach, what the magazine will or will not accept from freelance writers, and its editorial seasons and lead times. After that, consider the unique spin (the perspective from which you approach a story) you'll put on an old topic, the research and facts you'll need to back up your statements, and the experts you'll want to locate to add credibility to your topic. Seems like a lot of work for something you could do in your sleep, doesn't it?

Career Ups and Downs

If you are still leaning toward the theory that magazine writing might be easy, think again. Each time one of your submissions lands on an editor's desk, the odds are well over 90 percent that you'll be rejected, and there is nothing easy about that figure. It will cost you anywhere from just under to well over a dollar to make each pitch, and there's nothing easy in that statistic, either.

The major magazine writing pros and cons aside, however, there are still great reasons to be a freelancer, not just in magazines, but in any writing discipline:

- You are making a living doing the thing you most love to do.
- You control your working hours.
- You select the topics about which you'll write.
- You don't have to leave home or dress up, and you can take extra-long lunch hours.
- Your office space is your own, with no outside rules.
- You are free to schedule vacation time minutes in advance.
- There's no office gossip, because you are working alone.

Of course, there is a downside, too:

- Rejections mean no paychecks, meaning no electricity, meaning no computer, meaning you can't produce work that will generate a paycheck.

- You are responsible for all the phases of running your business, from buying paper clips to paying taxes.
- Equipment failure comes out of your own pocket.
- There's no one around to take the blame but you.
- There's no office gossip, because you are working alone.

Every freelancer has ups and downs in his career. Sometimes the work pours in, but at others it just trickles. And at other times, unfortunately, there are droughts. The good thing about writing for magazines is that the droughts can be overcome through hard work. There are more than 20,000 periodicals being published regularly in North America, and of these more than 75 percent accept 4 to 6 freelance articles per issue. Granted, some may offer only a few dollars per project, but a few dollars will help pay a bill.

Many magazine freelancers who have seen moderate success make the mistake of ignoring the magazines with low pay, even in times of drought (and yes, even the best magazine writers experience an occasional drought). Adopting the philosophy that any writing is good writing, however, can make the difference in whether you're living only on boxed macaroni and cheese this month or able to throw a little meat and some fresh vegetables into the mix. A noted speaker at writing seminars has an impressive list of publications, one anyone would envy. But he experiences droughts too, and in those times he writes obituaries. It's good work and it pays his bills, but he'd rather cut off an index finger than let anyone know what he's doing. Any writing is good writing if it pays the bills and doesn't go against your moral values.

Can You Turn a Lull Into an Advantage?

A writer who needs to make a living, or needs to write just to satisfy the urge, will go after the small jobs when his writing career is stalled. He will either create opportunities or dig out ones no one else knows are there. He will double his querying efforts, inquire about freelancing for his local newspaper (called being a stringer), spend more time at the library reading magazines he never knew were in print, and call editors who have published him before to ask about work. A true writer looks to the local weekly newspaper or shopping guide as a way to keep on writing, even though those publications rarely pay. He keeps his skills sharp by volunteering his writing services to a charity or a civic or community group, because he knows he cannot afford to be idle too long or he'll go rusty.

Is this something you could, or would, do when your career slows down? Or would you rather go watch a basketball game or bake a cake during your allotted writing time and wait to start writing again until a job presents itself?

One aspiring writer who could not get her own career going decided to do some volunteer writing for a victims' rights organization. Soon she moved into newspaper editorials, then magazine articles on the subject. Now she is a full-time magazine freelancer, thanks to the experience that came out of her writing lulls.

Learning From Your Lulls

Establishing a daily writing routine is a good way to strengthen your writing when you're not getting published. It might be easy to ignore your computer when nothing is happening to you professionally, but don't. Block out the time when you would normally write, and write. Put together an article you would really like to see published. Let your secret desire to write a cowboy novel get you started in that direction. Write the poetry that's been begging to get out.

It doesn't matter what you write as long as you do write. Practice really does make perfect, and the more you write, the better you'll become. To prove the point, look at something you wrote last year, then compare it to something you did last week. Which is better?

So keep writing, and while you're at it save some time to read. Naturally, the best things to read are articles similar to what you would like to write, in magazines in which you would like to be published. Read them with a writer's eye, evaluating them for both style and content. Then ask yourself the following questions:

- Did the writer prove the point he was trying to make?
- Did the style add to or detract from the message?
- Did the writer tell me everything I wanted to know, or would I have liked more?
- Overall, was it a good or a bad article?
- What needed more work?
- What didn't need to be there?
- What did I especially like?
- What did I especially dislike?
- What would I do the same way if I were to write that article?
- What would I do differently?

Eventually, most of your reading will be through a writer's eye. This is as natural as a chef evaluating every bite he eats in a restaurant other than his own, because it's human nature to check out the competition to see where they're beating you and you're beating them. Looking through a writer's eye is a learning process: You learn what's getting published and what's not. You are seeing the final result, as it has been edited by the editor, and are seeing an editor's preferences.

Maintaining Individuality and Still Fitting the Mold

Contrary to what many magazine editors say, they have molds they like to fill. Some editors expect a story heavy on anecdotes (a short account, usually personal or biographical, about something of interest) and light on facts, while others want the facts and perfer to skip the anecdotes. You'll come across editors who like meaty statistics and others who wouldn't touch a statistic with a ten-foot typewriter ribbon. Editors have story and writing-style preferences and definite fondnesses for openers and sidebar materials (a boxed section in an article that offers highlights, resources, or information that parallels the article but does not fit into the body). All these preferences and fondnesses are indicators of the way the editor writes. If you were the editor, wouldn't you prefer a style that resembles your own? Of course you would, and editors are the same. That's an editor's mold. Most editors would deny this, but seasoned writers will agree that many editors work hard to put their own touch on everything they edit.

An editor for one of the top women's consumer magazines once offered a writer an assignment on making money from hobbies. Everything was spelled out in the contract, with which the writer carefully complied. However, the writer had not seen the editor's work prior to writing for her, and the finished product turned out to be miles from what the editor wanted. Apparently, this editor liked list articles—articles that list the basic facts. The writer didn't do a list the first time but might have, had he known the editor's preference. Because most editors do write for their magazines, when you receive an assignment ask for copies of articles written by your editor and also request a few she has edited.

Giving your editor what she wants is important, but it is also important to you as a writer to maintain some of your own identity in your work. You do need those unique writing angles that separate your work from everything else, but you have to merge them with your editor's expectations. Maybe you have a great angle on presenting statistics but your editor hates statistics. Can you give your editor what she wants—no statistics—but still squeeze the ones you want into the piece? Sure, you can compromise. Choose the most important ones and let the rest go. Are you able to insert an anecdote you do not like, even though the editor has handed it to you on her silver platter? Compromise. Use your own words and be concise, so the anecdote doesn't take up more of the word count than you want to use.

At times you'll be stuffed into the editor's mold, like it or not. But to answer one of the most frequently asked questions at writing seminars—"For whom do I write?"—for the purpose of making a living you write for your editor. She is your boss and is the one who authorizes your paycheck. Most writers would like to say they are writing for themselves, which is an idealistic notion that artists in most fields maintain. It's admittedly nice to create only for the sake of creating, only for the sake of pleasing yourself. But when you want to be paid for that creativity you are writing for your editor. Normally, most editors will let you have your own space in their molds, but if they do not, so be it. The next time you work for that editor, her mold won't be so rigid because she has seen what you can do. And the time after that will be even better.

So, all things considered, do you have what it takes to be a magazine writer? The answer is that no one can tell you the answer. Persistence, energy, and curiosity will get you closer to your goal, as will dogged determination. But do you go after every bit of knowledge that will advance your career? And are you capable of working for your career even when your career is not working for you? Can you fill the mold and stay patient until you have your own space in it? In spite of all the ups and downs, can you still face your writing and say "I love this job" and mean it?

Only you know for sure if you have what it takes to be a magazine writer, but you won't really know until you give it a try, will you?

2
Points to Ponder

In life, as in chess, forethought wins.
—Sir Thomas Fowell Buxton

ALONG THE road to a writing career you will be faced with many decisions that will sooner or later have a bearing on that career. At the beginning, when your focus is on gathering information that will help you get published, you probably won't give much thought to matters such as using a pen name, whether to establish a niche for yourself or be a generalist, what category of article you want to write, or the type of magazine in which you would like to be published.

Magazine writing is full of matters that are as important as the writing itself. As you progress through your career you may find that decisions on such matters that you made at the beginning, when you were less experienced, are having a direct bearing on where you are finding yourself later on. These matters are points all magazine writers need to ponder in that giving them some early thought could head off problems down the road.

Pen Names

A pen name, or nom de plume or pseudonym, is a device widely associated with people who write books. Go find a novel, look at the author's name on the front cover, and see if it matches the name of the copyright holder. The law requires authors to copyright their work under their legal, or company, name, and when that copyright name differs from the name on the front cover the author is writing under a pen name.

Pen names have several purposes. The first is privacy—it allows an author to maintain her real identity. Second is for publication reasons: If an author is doing more than one type of writing, she may use different names for different forms of writing. The best-selling author Nora Roberts uses her own name on her romance novels, but her side career as a writer of detective and crime fiction comes under the name J. D. Robb. That way, when you purchase a book under the name Roberts or her alter-ego, Robb, you know what you'll be getting.

For the record, legally you own your name, and there is nothing a book publisher can do about that. Years ago, however, when a publisher issued a contract, a standard clause provided that the publishing company could also own your name. This was done to prevent a successful author from changing publishing companies and taking her name along, even if it was her own. An author had the right to leave at the end of the contract, but the name didn't. Today many publishers do own pen names, especially to particularly successful series. Carolyn Keene of Nancy Drew fame and Franklin Dixon of the Hardy Boys series are publisher-owned pen names under which dozens of men and women are writing.

By now you may be asking yourself what all this has to do with writing for magazines, especially when magazine by-lines (the name under which an article will appear) are rarely noticed, and magazine editors do not really care about the name you use. The answer is simple. Magazine pen names serve the same purposes as those used on books. They provide the writer with a measure of privacy, allowing her to pursue several categories of writing without confusing readers.

They also allow writers to conceal their gender, especially in gender-associated magazines and writing specialties. Outdoor sportsman magazines, for instance, are read largely by men who hunt and fish, and how many of them would give credence to, or even read, an article on new technology in hunting weapons written by someone named Debbie? Conversely, how many women would read an article on eyeshadow written by a writer called Howard?

While there are obvious benefits associated with using a pen name, there is also a problem concerning the recognition that may become attached to your name. Editors do remember some names that come across their desks in query letters, and they notice bylines in other publications. When the name on a query is associated with a byline they've read in another magazine, this connotes a track record and creates a sense of credibility and success. Editors occasionally approach writers in competing magazines to do similar stories, and if they cannot track you down because you are using a pen name, you could lose a good opportunity.

Using a pen name is a matter of choice, but if you decide to do so, pick one wisely, because the decision could stay with you for years to come. Consider the image you are trying to create. A business writer might select something short with a no-nonsense ring, like Al Bennett. A writer for a southern lifestyle magazine might choose something flowery, long, and descriptive, such as Savannah Beaujolais. Many writers devise a combination of family names, a nickname, or a variation of their own name. The use of first and middle initials is also popular, if they have a nice flow when put together. Certainly, Xerxes Walter—X. W.—wouldn't be a good choice, but Dianne Lyn—D. L.—would be.

In choosing a pen name, make sure it is not that of another famous writer, because most writers who have achieved success with a name register it as a trademark with the Library of Congress. Check a Library of Congress directory online or in your local library to make sure the pen name you would like to use isn't already registered to someone else.

After you've selected a name, live with it for a while before you commit to adopting it. Try several variations on the theme, and experiment with the spelling. Type it on your word processor to make sure it rolls off the fingertips easily. Doodle it on a legal pad to see how it looks in script and how easy it is to write. Look at yourself in the mirror and say it aloud, to see if the name as pronounced fits the face you are seeing. Ask someone to call you by that name, because, inevitably, you will be called by it on more than one occasion and it's always good to respond to the name by which people expect you to react.

As soon as you know you like a certain pen name, assume that identity. Now you and your pen name are one and the same.

Finding Your Article Category

The clothes you choose or the way you comb your hair show a preference, as does the type of article you prefer to write. Some people lean toward their article choice naturally, by virtue of their interests, education, or expertise, while others find what suits them by trial and error or dabbling with a little bit of everything until the perfect match finally manifests itself.

You wouldn't buy a bucket of paint and a paintbrush without knowing what you were about to paint, and the same goes for magazine writing. You don't sit down and start writing without knowing what you are writing.

Magazine articles fall into several broad categories. There is a huge difference between writing a Q & A piece and a personal essay. If you don't know the difference, or understand what is meant by a round-up piece or a list, it's time to look at the basic magazine categories in which freelance writing is accepted.

1. *As-told-to* stories are related by someone who has had an interesting life experience to someone who can record that experience. The basic premise is that the person with the experience is probably not a

writer but has a story worth writing up. Such an article is written in the first person, as if the teller is also doing the writing, and credit is given to the teller, with a mention of that subject's name, usually in a form similar to, "By (the subject) as told to (the writer)." In this case the writer, not the subject, receives the paycheck. As-told-to articles are popular in magazines that want true-life stories of real people facing overwhelming odds and accomplishing tremendous goals.

2. *Children's stories,* both fiction and nonfiction, are written for children, not about children, unless the target audience is adults. Children's articles fall into similar categories as articles found in magazines geared toward adults, but because children's writing is so specific to the reader's gender and age, the category often stands alone. Many writers have a mistaken notion that writing for children is easy. Some even assume that because they may be having a difficult time succeeding in the adult markets, they can drop down and give the children's markets a try. The truth is that writing for children is difficult, often more so than writing for adults, because of the narrow audience you are trying to reach. More than that, since the market is so specific, children's editors are among the most highly selective in all the magazine world. Writing for children can be tremendously rewarding, though, when you consider the impact you can make on a developing mind. Unfortunately, the biggest drawback for a freelancer trying to make a living in children's magazines is that the pay is low.

3. *Departments,* the short items that appear under the same heading every month, are a good way for new, inexperienced writers to break into magazines. They give an editor a chance to see a writer's style without committing to a full feature, and they offer a writer the chance to prove herself. These items' word counts are low, generally under 1000 per article, whereas features run an average of 1,500 to 2,500

words, but the pay per word is close to the pay for features. And having several department successes can result in a shot at writing a full feature, especially if the department editor keeps coming back to you for more work. Because writers do not flock to departments and columns, magazines usually have openings there for interested writers.

4. *Expository writing* takes current topics, news items, and newly discovered information and turns them into salable articles that explore all aspects of an issue. The dictionary defines expository as "a setting forth of facts, ideas, etc.; detailed explanation; writing or speaking that sets forth or explains." Topics can be diverse—anything from assisted suicide to claiming a downtown property by eminent domain. One thing an expository piece is not, however, is an opinion piece. Expository works offer facts; opinion pieces offer opinions based on the facts. Don't confuse the two.

5. *Fiction* is published in some magazines, but in the larger magazines that once traditionally ran fiction stories the frequency is declining because reader demand has turned to information. Often, in the larger magazines that still publish fiction, the space allotted for a fiction story (every editor is given a space allotment for each issue of the magazine) is taken up by best-selling book authors excerpting a new novel for the sake of publicity. This doesn't mean that all is bleak for magazine fiction writers, however. There are opportunities in children's magazines, entertainment tabloids, true crime and detective magazines, science fiction, fantasy and horror publications, true love and confession magazines, sexual fantasy publications, and a whole host of magazines that are not necessarily the best-sellers.

One more note on publications that especially welcome fiction: If you write fiction, poetry, or experimental forms of fiction, literary magazines could be the place to get your start. Literary magazines have small circulations, are rarely sold on newsstands, and often do not accept advertising. Because work published in literary magazines is considered to be intelligent, many book editors and agents seeking the kind of literary voice not usually found in mainstream magazines read the literary magazines. Check the current *Writer's Market* for literary listings, or browse a university library's periodical shelves.

6. *Fillers* are a great way to make a little extra money and build beginning writing credits at the same time. These are short nonfiction items, usually just under 300 words, to fill out a newspaper or magazine page.

7. *How-to* articles are among the most popular today. They teach the reader how to do something: how to protect a child from a virus, how to plant a high-yield, low-maintenance garden, how to find the right mortuary, how to have better sex. How-to articles cover almost any topic and are a favorite among readers because they deal largely with self-improvement and do-it-yourself projects. As a how-to writer it's your duty to ask, "How can I help my reader?" and then answer the question in article form.

8. *Human interest,* or true-life articles are similar to as-told-to articles, except here you are approaching the story as your own, reporting an interesting life story or dramatic event from your own perspective. These stories are designed to touch the hearts of people, to inspire them through events transpiring from the situations of others, to keep them on the edges of their chairs throughout the reading, and to relate stories that make readers glad they took the time to read them.

9. *Interview articles* come in many forms, the most basic being the question & answer (Q & A), where you ask the question and your subject answers it. Generally, these articles are published in the question-followed-by-answer format and cover one precise topic. The questions should always be prepared ahead of time. Here's a sample.

Writer: When was the first time you knew you wanted to be a poet?

Subject: I was six, and I wrote a poem about a pony I had just ridden. After that, the poetry came from everywhere. I even wrote a poem about the way my grandmother could take a simple food and turn it into ambrosia.

Writer: What did she think of it?

Subject: I don't know. She died before she had the chance to read it.

In a sense, the as-told-to format is an interview article, because you are writing an article based on what another person is telling you, and you may be required to ask questions to fill in the gaps and keep the flow going smoothly. These questions will be dictated by what the subject says, however, not structured as in a Q & A interview.

A third type of interview format article is the celebrity interview. This is structured in much the same way as a straight Q & A piece except that the questions can cover both personal and professional aspects of your subject's life instead of a single topic.

10. *List* articles are no-nonsense lists of facts: "Fifty-five Ways to Hazardproof Your Home" or "Ten Ways to Organize Your Hectic Mornings." In content they are similar to the how-to article except that the how-to will cover details of the theme, whereas the list article will highlight helpful tips and just give the bare-bone facts.

11. *Op-eds* (meaning opposite the editorial page, not opinion editorials) were named because they run opposite the editorial page, usually as a response to current editorials and topical subjects. Political op-eds are the most common form, but the subject matter of this type is not limited to politics and can cover a wide range of topics, so long as it reflects items that are current and newsworthy.

12. *Personal essays* are one of the easiest pieces to write, which is one reason many writers envision a magazine career writing nothing but reflections on

their own life. Good personal essays are often hu-
morous, sometimes poignant, and always have a
moral or purpose to the story—something that can
inspire, teach, or uplift the reader. They express the
writer's point of view concerning an experience that
shaped or changed her life, highlighting the necessary elements and eliminating the mundane. Personal essays are full of thoughts and feelings,
reactions and human emotion.

13. *Potboilers,* meaning works that are produced with little
    effort in quick time, are designed to "keep the pot
    boiling" when you are busy with a main writing assign-
    ment but are in need of a little fast cash. They can be
    fillers, how-to tips, or any other short piece.

14. *Round-up articles* are something we read in most
    magazines but are not widely pursued by magazine
    writers. In short, a round-up piece presents a posi-
    tion, then backs up the statement with a round-up of
    experts and quotes. You've read them: "Five Former
    Models Talk about Eating Disorders," or "Three Top
    Financial Analysts Predict the Economy." The
    article's premise is a basic question, followed by
    three to five opinions regarding it.

15. *Service or consumer advice* pieces are by far the
    mainstay of the magazine industry and the most widely
    published type of article. This category incorporates
    elements from almost all the other magazine article
    formats and tells the reader something he should know
    to make life better: "Fly Rights: Disability Law in the
    Air" or "Your Bank's Hidden Fees Are Costing You Big
    $$$!" Service or consumer articles range from travel to
    medical to help in bed and are packed with up-to-date
    statistics, theories, information, examples from real life,
    expert advice, helpful hints, descriptions, lists, and
    resources for more information.

16. *Shorties* are similar to fillers, but they fall in the
    department category. These are short articles, ranging
    from 50 to 300 words, grouped together with three or

four more shorties on a similar topic, all appearing on one page under a common heading, such as health tips, beauty facts, or household hints.

17. *Technical, professional, and trade articles* are written for magazines that deal with specific occupations or professions. Almost every organized working endeavor, from teaching to woodworking to writing, has a publication offering advice and updates in the field. (See more on trade publications later in this chapter.)

You're still not sure what article category will suit you? Go over the list again and see if there are certain types for which you have a ready idea. Most likely, the first article ideas that spring to mind will be ones into which you can insert yourself as an expert, or ones that come from a personal point of view: an as-told-to from a friend, a personal essay or a human interest event you witnessed. While there is no easy way to start a magazine career and no guarantee that the magazine articles you would like to write will sell, articles that come from some form of personal experience often lead to a writer's first success. So begin by writing articles on topics you know so well you could discuss their deepest details in your sleep.

To Niche or Not to Niche

Now that you see that there is more than one category of article open for the writing, the next thing to consider is whether you want to be a niche writer (a writer who specializes in one area) or a generalist (one who will write almost anything). There are advantages and disadvantages to both choices, but in the beginning of a writing career most writers choose to be generalists, taking any assignments they can get until they build the reputation, and enough credits, to make their real choice. The exception is the writer who approaches writing as an expert, such as a proctologist who wants to write only on issues dealing with prostate cancer, or a high school social worker who chooses to write only about teen problems.

These writers probably do not have the intention of becoming full-time writers, and, logically, most magazines are interested only in their areas of expertise. After all, who wants to read a description of ten ways to extend your car's gas mileage written by a noted proctologist? This doesn't mean that starting off as an expert won't lead to other things, however, because it can, if you're an expert considering taking up writing as a career. The auto mechanic who will write about getting better gas mileage may choose as his next article car care in preparation for a road trip. That in turn could lead to an article on car comfort when you travel, and another about ways to entertain kids on the trip. Great destinations by car can follow, then great travel destinations in general, until voilà! The auto mechanic expert has turned into a travel writer.

One of the ironies of the writing life is that generalists often want the green grass on the niche side, whereas niche writers often look longingly over at the generalist's side of the fence. Whichever side of the writing fence you choose, weigh the advantages and disadvantages before you make a firm decision, because once you are known for a certain writing style or topic, it may stick with you for a long time.

The advantages of niche writing include the following:

- Many editors prefer hiring writers who have written on the topic before.
- Being known as an expert can give you a good start on your writing career.
- Prior knowledge of your writing specialty makes research easier.
- You may be able to compile several articles on one topic into a book.
- You may gain name recognition.

The disadvantages include the following:

- Limiting the scope of your writing could limit your income potential.
- Experts in one area are not always regarded as writers who are capable of writing on other things.

- Popular niche areas such as health, sports, fitness, and nutrition are hard to crack.
- Many niche writers struggle with boredom occasionally.

The advantages of being a generalist include the following:

- You can turn anything of interest into an article, no matter what the topic.
- You can approach a wider variety of magazines, thereby increasing your pay potential.
- Being known as a jack-of-all-trades has an appeal to editors who do not specialize in a single article category.
- You develop the skill to research anything.

The disadvantages of being a generalist include the following:

- There are more generalists than niche writers, and the competition therefore is stiffer.
- In the morning you may write about treatments for athlete's foot, then in the afternoon on dehydrating fruits and vegetables. Such a quick switch can be daunting, and some writers cannot make it easily.
- Name recognition rarely happens.

Chances are that at the beginning of your career you don't know whether you want to be a generalist or a niche writer, but this will come to you along the way. When it does, you may be the one peering beyond the writing fence to the other side, wondering if it's greener over there. One solution is to straddle the fence—compromising between niche and general writing. Find three or four topics that suit you, then stick to them. That way you can have all the advantages of both niche and generalist writing, without their obvious disadvantages.

Magazine Markets

After you've studied your article choices and weighed the pros and cons of being a generalist or niche writer, the next point to ponder is the actual magazine market. To think that a magazine is a magazine is a magazine will not advance your career, because of the approximately 15,000 publications open to accepting your work no two are alike. Pay scales vary. Their editorial requirements and policies are structured to fit the magazine and its demographics (the statistical base of the population that reads the magazine, specifically their age, sex, and reading preferences). And the willingness of different magazines to work with new and unpublished writers differs.

Maybe you will prove to be one of the lucky few who can grab a magazine off the checkout rack and decide that's where you want to be published, then snap your fingers and succeed. This does happen occasionally, but the more common situation is to grab a magazine, study it, and discover where it fits in relation to all the other magazines of its kind. Then you weigh the options, such as the pay and the experience required to write for it, before you even make an approach. All this is called knowing the magazine market. To be published, knowing the magazine market is as important as how and what you write. Most people seeking employment know something about the establishment they hope will hire them, and the same should apply to magazine writers. Without a basic understanding of the industry and its magazines' structure, it's like applying for a job as a tailor without knowing who needs those services.

The establishment you hope will hire you comes in three levels, each defined by the compensation it offers for writing.

The first, or bottom, level is composed magazines that do not pay, pay very little, or pay in copies of the magazine. These magazines have small circulations, often are distributed by subscription only, and are rarely sold on newsstands. In this category are literary magazines, many association publications, newsletters, and some hobby and craft publications. Local publications circulated on a small scale are also found on this level. Generally, any publication with a circulation of 1,000, give or take a few hundred, will be on this first level of the magazine market, but there are magazines with circulations of several thousand that fall into this category too. Romance-confession magazines with huge circulations offer only a few pennies a word. So do many children's magazines, including the perennial favorites *Jack & Jill* and *Humpty-Dumpty*.

Writing for magazines that offer little or no compensation is where many magazine writers start. There is a widespread assumption, however, that these publications are just waiting for your work because they are on the bottom of the list. Another assumption, that these magazines do not have the same stiff requirements as the better-paying magazines, follows the same line of thinking. Both assumptions are wrong. When you do not offer the best you have, you'll be rejected by these publications as quickly as by publications on up the line. Publication openings in the smaller magazines are in fact as tight and competitive as they are in the larger magazines, because many people use them as an entry point for their career. So all the standard rules still apply when you query or send a completed article.

The second level of the magazine pyramid consists of locals, regionals, nationals, trade journals focusing on a specific occupation or profession, like journalism, insurance, or farming, special interest, religious, children's, and craft and hobby magazines, and anything else that offers moderate compensation. This rate is usually defined as from ten to fifty cents a word. These magazines typically generate a steady circulation base, offer advertising, and have only a small editorial budget.

Trade magazines in particular are accessible to writers, because they are looking for exact information dealing with one occupation, and the scope of what they publish is limited. Many trade publications will buy an article based on knowledge first and writing second. As a result, the writer who has both the writing skill and a solid knowledge of the subject stands an excellent chance of being published.

The same goes for the craft and hobby magazines. One noted model railroad enthusiast pays for his expensive hobby with his articles, because he has the information the railroad hobby magazines need. If you are a quilting expert, write for the quilting magazines. If your hobby is crappie fishing, there's a magazine for you.

The third level of the pyramid is one every magazine writer wants to conquer: the top-paying national magazines, sometimes called slicks for the paper on which they are produced. Their pay ranges from fifty cents to a few dollars a word, and their circulations are in the hundreds of thousands to millions. These are the hardest markets to break into, because large national magazines already have a pool of writers they tap on a regular basis. Your *Writer's Market* will indicate the percentage of freelance opportunities in each magazine, but that number will not take into account the use of regular freelancers who have continuing work with the magazine as compared to the use of one-time freelancers who publish one time and do not have an ongoing relationship. One of the largest, most popular women's magazines claims to be about 80 percent freelance written, but that is deceptive because the magazine uses dozens of regular freelancers. In its home consumer department, seventeen feature articles are produced each year. The editor and associate editor of the department write a combined four articles, eight are assigned to two regular freelancers, and two are assigned to the newest regular freelancer in the lineup, so only three are up for grabs. This lowers the actual percentage for real freelance work to just below 18 percent, which is typical of most large national magazines. These publications rely on their regulars to fill the freelance slots, because their editors like to establish a relationship upon which they can rely, one they know will result in a good product.

Although the national markets are tight, this doesn't mean you cannot break in. If there are three open spots, one could go to you. When one of the regular freelancers leaves or her work becomes unacceptable, you might be tapped for a place in the lineup. This happens all the time and is what you want to happen to you, because the best job you can get as a freelancer is a regular one that pays you the best money. Don't let the pessimists convince you that you can't break into the national scene, though some will try. You will hear lecturers at writing workshops say it just can't be done, but this is only because they haven't succeeded in cracking those markets themselves.

The writing markets at all the levels of the pyramid are open to good writers who are persistent about approaching them. Realistically, you probably won't get published in *Cosmopolitan* your first time out the door, and you may not make it there the next year, or the year after that. But then you may. Who's to say, except the editor?

Right now, the points you are considering are definitely ponderous. They all have a major bearing on the career you want, and the choices are tough. Choosing a pen name, working as a generalist or niche writer, what to write, and where to submit it are things you might not have considered when you decided it was time to be a writer. Most people sit down with the exciting purpose of committing something important to paper but haven't even thought about choosing between a personal essay and a how-to.

In his *Rubáiyát*, the poet Omar Khayyám said, "The moving finger writes, and having writ, moves on." The object in magazine writing is not to move on, but to stay and find the career you want. With experience and a little staying power, the points you are pondering will become obvious choices. Everything will fall into a rightful place. But knowing ahead of time where those rightful places exist can be a big help in moving your career forward.

3
Getting Started

Let's start at the very beginning.
That's a very good place to start.
—Richard Rodgers and
Oscar Hammerstein II

EDITORS READ hundreds of queries and unsolicited manuscripts every week, and divide what they read into two categories: accepted and rejected. Accepted manuscripts distinguish themselves from those that are rejected not only in their writing form and subject, but in subtle ways—the research behind the piece, the technology involved in producing it, the way the writer deals with his editor. You may think one of your ideas is so good that it will catch the title position on the front cover of an upcoming edition, but when your query goes to the wrong editor to begin with, or your editor's eyestrain is so bad she can't distinguish the dots on your faint dot matrix printout, or you actually believed you could get away with penning your article on notebook paper, your article may never see the light of day, let alone the cover.

Actually, getting started is a difficult step in the process of becoming a magazine writer. You are now past the decisions concerning a pen name and the category of article you would like to write, but you're not quite ready for the writing. You may think you are, and may know your ideas are better than the ones you keep seeing over and over in magazines: "How to Lose Ten Pounds in Ten Days," "Drop a Pound a Day," or "One Week to a Whole New Body." So you could sit down, dash off that article that's been begging to be written, then keep your fingers crossed while you wait for your paycheck to arrive in the mail. But maybe it's time to look at some basic tools that will make your work better and more competitive.

Since you know that an editor's desk is stacked to the ceiling with work from other writers looking for their break just as much as you are, it's up to you to separate your work from everything else in the pile.

Your Personal References

Before proceeding, find a copy of *The Elements of Style* by William Strunk and E. B. White (the author of the classic *Charlotte's Web*). Absorb it, then make it the first contribution to your reference shelf. This book is widely considered the best reference on writing style. As a magazine writer, if you get nothing else out of it other than the prudent advice to "omit needless words" your money will have been well spent. Another book lining many personal reference shelves is William Zinsser's *On Writing Well: An Informal Guide to Writing Nonfiction.*

Most writers own a good dictionary, a thesaurus, and a grammar text, the fundamental tools of the job. If you don't own them, it's the same as a carpenter going to work without a hammer and nails. The editions you purchase do not have to be the latest. One noted author wouldn't be without Clement Wood's *Complete Rhyming Dictionary,* published fifty years ago, even though newer editions are on the market. Another writer wouldn't exchange her 1962 *Webster's New World Dictionary* for any other one out there.

In other words, what you choose is not as important as the fact that you do so. Go to a public or university library and browse the reference section to discover what you like.

Check it out and live with it for a while, or spend a few hours reading through it if it's a noncirculating book. Then check your local bookstores or an online source and make the purchase. When these references are finally in your hands, consult your thesaurus for a better word choice, look up a meaning in the dictionary just to verify that you are on the right track, and by all means make sure your participle isn't dangling. These are important distinctions that separate good writing from bad, published writers from unpublished.

Be aware that collecting references can become a habit after a while. A best-selling romance author noted for her collection has thousands of volumes in her own personal library. She claims she has never met a reference book she couldn't buy. While she may be an extreme case, most writers recognize the need for a few good references beyond the basics. For a freelance magazine writer to find work, the most valuable tool is a publication listing current magazines. Several are available, updated yearly and found in most libraries, including those of universities.

- *Writer's Market,* published by Writer's Digest Books, lists nearly 2,000 magazines with their editorial requirements for being published.
- *The National Directory of Magazines,* published by Oxbridge Communications, contains more than 20,000 magazine listings.
- *The International Directory of Little Magazines & Small Presses,* from Dustbooks, lists about 6,000 markets.
- *Editor & Publisher International Yearbook,* published by BPI Communications, is a good source for writers interested in newspaper freelancing. So is *Newspapers Online* from BiblioData.
- *Gale Directory of Publications and Broadcast Media,* published by Gale Research, is also a good source for freelancers looking for different opportunities.
- Trade magazines such as *Writer's Digest* and *The Writer* also carry market listings.

Whenever you rely on any serial volume (a book that is updated and reissued each year), recognize that anything included in it is outdated, although not necessarily obsolete, by the time it reaches your hands. Normally, the information you read in a serial work is at least a year old, and sometimes even more, depending upon how long it took the publisher to fact check and compile the book. The directories given earlier are good starting places, but do not rely on them as the final authority. You should make yourself the final authority when you take the information contained in a volume, such as an editor's name or the magazine's current address, and do your own fact checking by calling the publication to verify that information.

Good writing references will make a difference in your career, but remember one thing as you read them (and that includes this book)—not everything you read will work for every writer. A magazine writer makes his own way in the industry; the writing references used to get there are merely basic tools.

Keeping Up with the Technology

There's a not-so-old movie starring Chevy Chase called "Funny Farm," in which Chase's character moves to the New England countryside to write a novel. There he encounters distractions that prevent his writing, but his intrepid wife, who has a hidden desire to be a writer, starts her own book. She pens it on a yellow legal pad, sends it in, and receives a typed copy of her manuscript back in the mail a few weeks later, along with a check. This is a nice fantasy, but the publishing industry does not work that way. Handwritten manuscripts on legal pads are rejected. Today even faint dot matrix printing is rejected.

There is now an industry standard that all magazine writers must follow if they want to succeed. First is the computer, or word processor. Typewriters are for present purposes obsolete, because publishers want a disk, and often an electronic submission. For writers who can expect to be going against a deadline regularly, being able to e-mail an article at the last minute can be a blessing. A decade ago, e-mail didn't matter. Today you can query by e-mail in some cases, submit your manuscript, and correspond with your editor by e-mail. For a writer trying to keep up with the industry, e-mail is an important piece of technology.

Your choice of a writing program is not quite so important, as long as you do not use something so outdated that your editor cannot translate your work into her computer format. But your printer choice is important. Most dot matrix printing is not acceptable anymore, unless it is the very best letter quality. Inkjets and laser printers are preferred.

What about a facsimile, or fax, machine? Do you really need one? The answer is yes. Editors correspond by fax, information for research on an article can come via fax, and contracts and edited copies of manuscripts are faxed. A wealth of state and federal government information is available from a fax-on-demand source listed in the government section of your phone book. Virtually every magazine editor you will encounter has a fax, and most editors will assume that you have one. You don't need a fancy plain-paper machine that does everything but cook dinner; a cheap thermal-paper model will do. And you do not need to hook your fax up to a dedicated line—a telephone line used only for your fax machine. Once you become a full-time, forty-hour, five-days-a-week magazine writer working on several projects at a time, having a separate fax line might be wise, but until then hook your fax up to your regular phone line to save money.

An inexpensive answering machine is a good investment, too. Many people prefer voice mail, which has the advantage of taking your calls when the phone line is busy. But for a writer on a tight budget, an answering machine does the job. Whatever you choose, just make sure you have something picking up your calls, because editors work in all time zones and you never know when a call will come in.

A computer or word processor, a good writing program, a good printer, e-mail, a fax, and an answering machine are hardly the legal pad and pencil, but they are tools used by most successful magazine writers. More than that, they produce the results editors expect. This doesn't mean that if you can produce a good result on a typewriter or an outdated computer you should trade them in on something better. What it does mean is that magazine writing is a competitive business, and to succeed all freelancers need every edge they can get. One huge advantage comes with having good technology. If you can't afford a computer and your typewriter has some missing keys, many copy centers, libraries, and universities make computer time available at a small cost. The same goes for fax machines: Copy centers and office supply stores make such services available, also at a small cost. With e-mail so popular, probably you have a friend who has the computer capability, so work out a deal with him for your own e-mail account.

The bottom line is that there are ways to achieve a professional look through the technology editors expect, if you want it badly enough. It may not be right at your fingertips, but the writing life will not always be easy or convenient.

What Does the Magazine Want?

For the price of two first-class stamps, you can receive an instruction sheet defining exactly what a magazine wants in an article. Called its guidelines, it will tell you what areas of the magazine are open to freelancers and which types of articles the magazine requires. Send a short letter to the magazine asking for its guidelines, making sure you enclose a legal-sized self-addressed stamped envelope (known as a SASE).

Before you query a magazine, check its guidelines. What you have in mind may be perfect but might not fit at all. Then search the library for both current and back issues, studying them to see what the magazine is publishing, what it has already published, and, most of all, whether your article will fit the magazine.

Your idea might be the most exciting thing to come along in decades, but if it doesn't fit the magazine you are targeting it will be rejected . You cannot expect an article on California's wine country to fit the pages of a cat fancier magazine, and an article about a cat certainly won't be accepted in an exercise magazine unless your cat is adept at aerobics.

One of the most common complaints from editors is reading queries that are not right for their magazine. You will see this mentioned in rejection letters: "Your submission does not fit the magazine," or "Read the guidelines!" A more subtle way of saying you missed the target is to enclose a set of guidelines with the rejection. The way to avoid such rejection is to read the magazine and study its guidelines. If you cannot find the magazine anywhere, most publishers make back issues available for a few dollars. Call the publisher and ask the price, send for the sample, and then study it. Nothing says "professional writer" better than a focused query that hits its target.

Finding the Right Idea

What is the right idea? Every magazine editor is on a perpetual hunt for it, but the definition of "right idea" is elusive. The right idea is something not seen before by the editor. The right idea is also something she sees all the time. The right idea is one that is always popular with the reader, no matter how many times it has been published in the past. The right idea is____. Fill in your own definition here, because no one knows what the right idea is or will be until your editor looks at it and says "yes." Chances are your editor doesn't even have a firm definition of the right idea until it springs from your query letter and grabs her.

An unchanging fact of magazine writing is that certain topics always sell. Another certainty is that editors don't move too far away from their proven winners. Check two or three popular magazines at your favorite newsstand. Do you recognize the cover stories? They sound like the same old rehashed articles you read last month, and the month before, don't they?

Sure they do. But there are just as many new ideas that can grab an editor's attention too, so when you're thinking about an article you'd like to write, the better choice is always one the editor doesn't include in the pages of her magazine every other month. The catchwords most editors use to describe the elusive idea are "fresh and original." In other words, they want something they haven't seen before. How can you find this evasive little concept?

- *Stay alert.* Ideas come from anywhere—a friend, a stranger, television, a conversation from the next booth over, a Sunday sermon, your children, a billboard, your own job or your best friend's job, your neighbor's dog, your last vacation, your divorce. Everything you hear or see has the potential to be a magazine article idea, so keep yourself tuned in to your surroundings. Read, listen, observe, remember.
- *Be prepared.* Always keep a notepad and pen handy to catch an idea as it happens. A small tape recorder will work, too.
- *Be bold.* Strike up a conversation and ask questions when you hear a good idea. Get facts and details. Call the 1-800 number you saw advertised and ask for more information. Send away for that free brochure.

Consult the *Reader's Guide to Periodical Literature,* published by H. W. Wilson, for ideas already in print. Older volumes of this resource will list articles dating back over 100 years.

In a writer's world everything you experience can serve as the beginning of a magazine article—everything, that is, except the article you just read in another magazine. One huge mistake many writers make is assuming that such an article has the potential for being a great article in another magazine, then sending off a query to it. Competing magazines are aware of what their rivals are publishing and in many cases may even have rejected the story you thought was so great. So don't make the mistake of finding your ideas in competing magazines. An editor will spot this right away, and you'll soon earn the reputation of being unable to produce an original topic. Two or three queries based on competitors' articles, especially current articles, could cause an editor to disregard your work altogether. Two or three queries on topics an editor has never seen, however, can be just what you need to start you on the road to success.

How do you know if you are pitching a topic the editor hasn't seen? There's no way of knowing for sure, but you can guess that anything that's trendy at the moment or has made the news recently has been queried dozens of times. Anything that's so old it's become ordinary has no doubt wandered through an editor's query pile, too. This doesn't mean that you can't use these ideas, however. You can, as long as you put a new spin on them. Instead of writing about the problems caused by iron deficiency, write about those associated with too much iron in the blood. Instead of writing about better ways to utilize your food coupons, write about outlet or online grocery shopping.

A final word on finding your ideas. Be wary of what you pull off the Internet. An idea might sound good, but you must do your own research to make sure it is a legitimate contender for a magazine article. When you query an idea you find on the Internet, back it with primary research—original research or facts that come directly from the source—not secondary research, something another journalist has written about the topic. The Internet provides a tremendous amount of unregulated, uncontrolled information, which is often questionable or inaccurate. Remember that since the Internet is an easy source of ideas, many writers are using it, probably pitching the same idea you just discovered and have decided to pitch too.

Researching Your Topic

Research is the backbone of any good article. It defines your ability as a writer and tells an editor you are capable of composing a piece that is more than something off the top of your head. Unless you are writing an opinion piece or any form of personal story, an article must contain facts, figures, statistics, and any other current information that will make it valuable to a reader. Who cares about, say, reading an article on the rise of breast cancer if the writer fails to prove that the disease is actually on the rise? Without hard research backed by the latest facts and statistics, the article is nothing more than words on paper that do not prove a point.

There are three basic rules of research. First, research must come from the most current sources. Old or outdated information is of no use to your reader and is a clear indicator to your editor that you didn't do your homework.

Second, research must be from the primary source. In a recent case, several magazines reported that 80 percent of all female athletes suffered from iron deficiency. The actual incidence was half that, but the original source of the information was incorrect. Even worse, at least ten other magazine writers came up with the same statistic, not because they had checked it at its primary source but because they had relied on the information gathered by another journalist, who was the secondary source of the information. One of the biggest mistakes a magazine writer can ever make is to assume that everything he reads in another article is correct. The only way to know for sure is to check the information at its source of origin.

Third, research must be verifiable. Magazines employ fact checkers, who do nothing but check the pertinent facts in articles. If you make them up or cannot produce your sources, you won't be published.

The library is always a good place to start your research. A basic physiology book will acquaint you with anemia if you are pitching a query on the disease. After that, consult other periodicals for your topic—not so you can use their secondary facts, but to see where they gathered their information. Many articles will list resources to contact for more information, and it's perfectly acceptable to check them. Look through a copy of *National Trade and Professional Associations of the United States* (Columbia Books). If your topic happens to be one that has a national association connected to it, call that group for information and ask for a referral to experts you can interview. (See more about finding experts in Chapter 4.)

The first line for research is your library, so you should get to know it:

- Is your library a government repository for documents?

- If you do not have personal access, does your library have access to online data banks?
- What kind of microfilm stores does your library have?
- Do you have a specialty library in your area, such as a law library or a dental library?
- How far is it to the nearest university library?
- Does your local newspaper allow public access to old editions?
- Is there a library in your local hospital?

Find out the answers to these questions, browse a while, then strike up a friendship with a librarian, who can be a valuable assistant to a writer. The Romance Writers of America, a professional writing association, recognizes the role a good librarian can play in the research process and presents a yearly national award to an outstanding librarian. Many top authors actually employ librarians to assist in their research. So make their acquaintance and let them know you are a writer doing your research, but don't rely solely on them. Explore your library's nooks and crannies to learn for yourself what's there.

Research also comes from sources such as newspapers, the Internet, television, and other media. These sources of information are usually secondary ones, but they can lead you to primary sources. Call the reporter and ask for more information when something catches your eye in a newspaper article or television report. You may not pick up the primary source from these people, because good journalists guard their sources, but you may gather information that will lead you to it. Or you can call the person who was interviewed. For example, if you're watching a national broadcast and you see an interview with a Dr. Smith, he will be identified in some way, usually in a caption under the picture: "Dr. Allen Smith, Professor of Zoology at Emory University, Atlanta." That's all you need to find him—call the university in Atlanta. If you don't get enough information to locate him, call the network or station and ask. You'd be surprised how much information is easy, accessible, and just waiting to be found.

The same advice goes for the Internet. When something intrigues you, contact the person or organization posting it and ask about its source. You may learn nothing, but again you may find out everything you need.

Good journalists never leave a research stone unturned. They go after anything that looks potentially useful. Granted, many leads are dead ends, but just think what could happen if you become the one to find the research that proves that the iron deficiency rate in female athletes is actually 35 percent instead of 80. That's good research, which gets an article published.

Evaluating Your Article's Sales Potential

Before you approach an editor, first evaluate your article's potential for the magazine you are targeting. Ask yourself these five questions, and be objective with your answers:

1. Is it a nationally relevant story, or something that will appeal only to readers in Houston, Texas, or Kalamazoo, Michigan?
2. Is it really worthy of a feature story, or can it be used in a smaller capacity, such as a filler?
3. Who will find this article appealing and relevant, and are they the people who read the magazine I intend to target?
4. Does the magazine I'm targeting publish this kind of article?
5. Has the magazine I'm targeting published a similar article in the past three years? (Magazines recycle topics every three to five years, so there is no need to check issues older than three years.)

After you've answered these questions, extend your objectivity a bit more and ask yourself, Is this topic one I would read myself if I weren't the writer? When you approach a story, you have to build up a certain amount of enthusiasm for it, and if you've chosen a topic that doesn't excite or even interest you, the writing can become pretty difficult, and this will show in your final product. What makes you think others will want to read a story written by you when you wouldn't care to read the same story written by someone else? Choose a topic you would read and you will be writing something others will want to read too.

Now consider the perspective of your story before you make a pitch to an editor. Have you come up with the best way to present your idea? Are there other ways that might work better? One enthusiastic beginner at a writing conference saw three different participants, with injuries, walking on crutches. Because he'd been on crutches for a time years before, he envisioned an article about walking on crutches. He pitched it dozens of times, but it did not sell, so he finally gave up. The truth was that the article was nothing more than a list of four people's experiences walking on crutches, personal stories that dealt as much with why they were on the crutches as with the physical act of coping with the crutches. There were no tips on better ways to use crutches or how to get along in a crowd. Neither were there any funny stories relating to life with an extra couple of legs. Had the writer changed his approach to the story, he might have made a sale. So in evaluating your idea before you send it off to an editor, ask yourself the final, and probably most important, question of all: Is this the best way to pitch or write my story, or can I come at it from a better angle?

Know Your Editors

The editorial structure of a magazine is important to the writer, because the editor is always the writer's boss. That, if nothing else, makes knowing your editor important.

It's not necessary to get to know your editor on a personal basis, especially if you're a freelancer from Nebraska and your editor is in New York. But knowing your editor's job, place in the magazine hierarchy, and overall authority and ability to make decisions will help you make the best choices in targeting an editor. As in targeting a magazine, you also target a magazine editor.

Make sure you are targeting an editor who is currently with the magazine. You can do this by calling and asking, or checking the masthead (the page listing the editorial staff, usually found near the beginning of the magazine) in the magazine's latest edition. Sending a query to one who is not listed—editors do move around—could bog down your query for weeks while any number of people read it and try to decide where it should go. A disturbing trend in the magazine industry today is that up to half of all queries are simply not answered, and half again are not answered in a timely fashion—that is, in one to two months. This makes finding the right editor even more important, because it is the best way to ensure that your submission is read and answered.

The Masthead

Unless the guidelines state otherwise or you've been told something different by an editor, there are editors you approach and ones you do not. Go grab a magazine and open it to the masthead. Magazines vary in their editorial staff positions, but here is a general guide to follow, starting at the top.

- The publisher, editor-in-chief, deputy editor, executive editor, and managing editor are the people vested with the responsibility of running the magazine, including all its editorial and business aspects. In large-circulation national magazines the magazine's managers are not the editors to query under normal circumstances. Ultimately, the final editorial decisions fall on this level of the magazine's editorial staff, not the initial decisions or responsibilities such as reading queries and investigating the possibility of turning a query into an article. In small magazines, however, where editors have a tendency to wear more than one hat, these people may be the editors to query. Find out from the guidelines, or call the magazine and ask.

- Articles editors, features editors, senior editors, and department editors (such as health and fitness, or fashion and beauty) are responsible for producing articles specific to their assigned job or section of the magazine. These editors write, edit, read queries, and make decisions on those queries. They also work with freelancers in producing articles. This level is a good one to query, but note that because editors of this rank have worked in magazines for a while, they are more likely to have established a list of regular freelancers. Still, they are the ones who make the decisions that start the editorial process, their decisions have clout with upper-level management, and good editors are always looking for good new writers.
- Associate editor is an interesting position halfway between the level of the magazine employee who has no editorial control at all and the level that has much of the control. Although an associate editor does not have complete authority over a project, she does much of the same work as the editors on the next level up, including reading and accepting queries, working directly with the writer, and editing the final work to make it ready for approval. While an associate editor is not vested with complete control over a project, there is an advantage to querying an associate. Editors on this level often do not have their list of regular writers established and are looking for a few good writers to help boost their career. They may thus be more open to working with beginning writers and writers new to the magazine.
- Editorial assistants and assistant editors rarely have editorial power, or the authority to make decisions. In some magazines they are assigned to read queries and pass along the good ones to an editor higher in the editorial structure, but this level of the editorial staff has little contact with the writer except in the capacity of assisting another editor. Unless the guidelines direct you to do so, do not query an assistant editor or editorial assistant.

- Contributing editors work for the magazine as part of the regular staff, but they usually specialize in a particular field of writing and editing. Often they are in charge of specialty departments and projects within their area of expertise. Contributing editors do have editorial authority and will read queries directed to their specific area of specialization. They are the ones to query when you hope to contribute to their editorial section.
- The research editor checks your facts, and the copy editor makes sure your article is in final form for printing. Research and copy editors are never queried.
- All the rest of the names on the masthead have little relevance to the writer. These are the people who produce and distribute the magazine, sell advertising, coordinate the art, serve as special advisors, and do a whole host of other jobs required to move the magazine from the concept stage into the hands of its readers.

If you've studied the masthead but still can't figure out which editor to target, call the magazine. Say, "I'd like to send a query on how to strengthen muscles without adding bulk. Could you please tell me the name of the editor to whom I should send this query?" Or, "Could you please tell me the name of the editor reading fitness queries?" Always ask how to spell the name, and if it is not obvious from the name, the gender of that editor. One New York editor's name appeared incorrectly for several years in one of the writers' directories, changing her sex from female to male, and she took full advantage of the error. When a query came in addressing her as a male, she rejected it automatically, because she knew that the writer had gone no further than the misinformation in the book. A query with her name spelled correctly was set aside for later consideration, because she knew that the writer had found her name on the masthead. But a query that came in using her nickname received an immediate read and response, because her nickname was the name given out when a writer took the time to call the magazine and ask. Granted, this is not a normal screening process for most editors, but the little things do count, including the proper spelling of the name and the right gender identification.

The Writer–Editor Relationship

A writer's good relationship with an editor may bring an opportunity to write more articles. An editor's good relationship with a writer may bring the opportunity to receive more articles. Basically, the writer–editor relationship is give and take, both doing a little of each.

In this relationship it is the writer's responsibility to give the editor the best work he can produce. This package includes the query, the article, the experts, and the facts to check. It is the editor's responsibility to make sure the article finds a spot in an upcoming edition, set up the standards and format for the article, and put it in the best form for the magazine, then execute the contract and authorize payment. This all seems pretty straightforward, at least when the relationship is working well, but what happens if you have a difference of opinion with your editor? In fact, are you even allowed to have a difference of opinion?

Begging to Differ

Disagreements do happen. It's pretty disheartening to visualize your article one way, then have your editor assign it in a completely different context. Your query may have focused on a broad spectrum of gastrointestinal disorders when your editor has eyes only for ulcers. Get used to it. More often than not, editors get their way. This is not necessarily a bad thing, because their overall goal is the magazine's total editorial picture, whereas yours is only one article. And this is not to say you can't disagree, because you can, but make it a controlled discussion. Be calm when you tell your editor what you have in mind and why you think what she is proposing might not work as well. Ask whether there is room for a compromise: Can you include some of your original information in a sidebar or another short article to accompany the larger article? Will your editor meet you halfway? Don't be too disappointed if she concedes only minor points or doesn't concede any at all. Your article may bear your byline, but it must reflect your editor's work too.

You'll be amazed at how things will twist and turn from your original concept of the idea to the completion of the project. The final cut of your article may turn out to be something not even close to what you proposed or wrote. A writer for many of the parenting magazines once did an article on celebrating baby's first Christmas or Hanukkah. The editors were thrilled with the piece and didn't even ask for rewrites. But imagine the writer's surprise when one section of the article turned out to be about the traditions of Kwanzaa. It wasn't a bad thing, just an unexpected twist thrown in, which happens. Editors see things differently than writers. The editor for the holiday piece saw a good query and accepted it, but later saw a hole in the article that she hadn't considered until she actually read it. In the best interests of her magazine she filled that hole.

Occasionally, coming to terms becomes an obstacle in the writer–editor relationship. That in turn becomes an obstacle in getting an article written. A new editor with a sports publication accepted a proposal from one of her predecessor's regular freelancers and gave out the assignment with instructions to follow the proposal exactly as written. But after the first draft, she decided that she wanted different experts quoted, part of the main body squeezed into a sidebar, and a different focus on the point of view. Because the editor was new at her job, the writer tried to persuade her that the changes would not work within the context of what the article was supposed to say, but the editor insisted, so the writer complied. Then the editor wanted more and more changes, until eventually she wound her way back to the original proposal and the original draft of the piece. When a second article with the same editor went the same way, the writer moved on, because working for an editor with whom one can never agree is not productive. Sometimes it's just not worth the effort.

Changing the Facts

Fact finding is a difficult subject to approach, because occasionally editors change or misinterpret facts. Normally, this is done in an effort to conserve word the count, but there are situations in which the editor has changed something only for the sake of change. Unfortunately, most editors do not allow the writer to view a final draft of the manuscript before it goes to press, so when the article is published, what the editor has done could be a big surprise.

There are two basic ways to handle this situation, but neither will guarantee that you won't be caught with words attributed to you that you didn't want.

First, ask for a look at the final, edited draft. You probably won't get it, but you never know.

Second, when you send your editor a manuscript, include a second copy with all the pertinent fact-checking information: sources for statistics and facts, and how your experts can be reached to verify their quotes. Indicate the areas of your manuscript that absolutely cannot be changed, and verify the spelling and gender of all your experts. Keep a copy of this fact-checking manuscript for yourself.

Editors are not malicious and will not change a manuscript to make you look bad. At the same time, however, all magazine writers have had manuscripts with editorial changes that embarrassed them. While that is a problem, it is not usually a serious one. There is one thing you need to know, however: You are the one liable for the content of your article. The magazine will assume no responsibility if someone wants to sue you. So if you are being sued over a portion of an article in which facts or quotes were changed by your editor, make sure you can prove that the words were not yours. On a brighter note, lawsuits against magazine writers are rare, and there are certain types of insurance policies, such as for errors and omissions, that will cover the situation. Talk to your insurance agent or lawyer to see if you even need the insurance, because you may not.

Editor Etiquette

Your editor will establish the ground rules for your relationship. For some editors this will always be a formal arrangement, while others may ask about your kids and want a detailed description of your last vacation when they call. Take your cue from your editor, but follow some ground rules of your own until you've figured it out.

- Always make a formal approach initially. Address your first correspondence to Mr., Ms., or Mrs. If return correspondence addresses you by your first name and your editor signs her first name, you can assume that it's okay to use that first name in the next correspondence. If she keeps the salutation formal, do the same.
- When the first phone conversation comes, stick to the formal usage, unless your correspondence has established a more casual relationship. An editor who starts with, "Hello, Mrs. Smith. This is John Jones, senior editor of *Your Favorite Magazine*," is probably going to stick to a formal tone. However, one who leads into a conversation with, "Hi, Sally. This is John Jones from *Your Favorite Magazine*, and I really liked your query" is trying to establish a more casual relationship. Again, take your editor's cue to distinguish between a formal and a casual conversation.
- Call an editor when you are working on an article and have questions, but never call to make a pitch over the phone if you do not have an established relationship. And even with a good relationship, make sure your editor doesn't mind phone queries.
- Don't expect an immediate response to your phone calls, e-mails, or faxes. Editors are busy people who are greeted with stacks of work every day. Wait a day or two, then try again.
- Don't let your editor down. When problems arise with your article, as perhaps an expert didn't come through

or the statistics do not after all support the premise, don't wait until the last minute to tell your editor. Let her know what's happening as far in advance as you can, and work on a solution to the problem. Editors have vast resources at their fingertips, and what might seem like an overwhelming problem to you could have a solution as close as your editor's Rolodex.

Now that you understand a little more about what it takes to get started—resources, technology, idea and research, and how an editor ticks—you've built the foundation for your career. This base will grow stronger as you learn and experiment to find what works best for you. Today, in the competitive magazine market no one is published without that foundation, and no one continues to be published over and over again without strengthening the things that helped them get published in the first place.

4
Query! Query! Query!

Things don't turn up in this world unless somebody turns them up.

—President James A. Garfield

IN THE MAGAZINE world, writing jobs don't turn up—unless you turn them up for yourself. You won't literally wear out your shoe soles making the rounds to every magazine publishing office trying to find that job, but you will wear out those soles figuratively by making the rounds in your query letters.

A query is a question, a big question: probably the most important one you will ask throughout your writing career.

May I write for you? Every published writer has asked this question, over and over. Every writer who hopes to be published also asks the question. If you don't ask it, things won't turn up.

A query is three things:

1. A job application.
2. A sales pitch.
3. An impression maker.

A query provides the information a future boss must know before he can hire you. It introduces your article idea, argues the case that you are the best person to write it, and allows you the opportunity to prove that you are the best writer. Most important of all, your query is the first impression you make on an editor. Some even say it's the most important writing you will do, because all the factors determining whether or not you'll get hired are based on what you put into your query.

You don't have to get dressed up and comb your hair to apply for the job. You don't even have to set an appointment. The beauty of a query is that you can write it at your convenience, when your idea is ready, your information is lined up, and you've done enough research to know which magazines might be interested in your work. But just because you can approach your query casually doesn't mean you should write a casual query. A query is a structured job application in which five questions every editor asks must be answered:

1. Who is this writer?
2. Why does this writer want to write this article?
3. What qualifies this writer to write this article?
4. What has this writer written before?
5. Can this writer write?

This chapter will explore the elements of a successful query, offer tips on how to make your query stand out among the rest, and tell you what editors want to see in a query letter and package. It will also encourage you to explore your own style, because to succeed every writer must develop an individual style. If you haven't found your own style yet, it will offer some basics that work.

Before You Start

Magazine editors are busy people. Their desks are piled with papers; reading queries and manuscripts is only a small part of their job. In large magazines they are responsible for the stories you browse while you're waiting in line at the grocery store, they make sure the art department does a respectable job with illustrations, and they attend editorial meetings where every accepted article and potential article is discussed in detail. In small magazines, editors do all of the above, plus check the facts in an article and issue the writer's paycheck. Their job is a complex variety of tasks that puts them on a deadline, just as they put you on a deadline. Queries and manuscripts are an editor's lifeblood when it comes to finding new material to publish every month, but reading them comes after their long list of other editorial responsibilities is completed. So when your query finally manages to grab twenty seconds of an editor's time it must separate itself from everything else in the stack to receive a good look, not just a passing glance from a busy person.

To get the most for your third of a minute of attention, your query must be three things:

1. *Focused.* You really do have just a few seconds to make your query count. If your letter rambles on about your family, what happened at work last week, or how you've always wanted to be a writer, you've told the editor that your writing wanders. As concise as magazine articles are today, writing that wanders does not get published.
2. *Brief.* One page maximum. It's the industry standard, but it also demonstrates that you can say everything that needs to be said in just a few words. Brief is how editors like articles to be written, too, and a brief query shows that you can do that.
3. *Professional.* Editors expect a professional draft, not a personal note, especially from writers they don't know. This isn't to say that at some point in your writer–editor relationship a personal note can't be used, because this does happen, but only after the editor knows you and your work. Until then, don't let your query be too chummy.

Clips

Clips are examples of your published work, usually from magazines and newspapers. Editors do read them to judge your writing style. Often a good clip will offset a query that does not
work. Most editors have a list of articles they need or would
like to see written. If an editor likes your clips but your query
doesn't fit his current needs, he might assign you a topic from
his list. If you don't have clips, though, don't worry. There are
ways to get published without them. But don't resort to sending copies of newsletters, church bulletins, and brochures you've
written, because editors do not want to see these. They want a
good look at articles you've written for publications similar to
theirs to determine whether your writing will fit into their pages.
And yes, editors do want proof that you've been published in
Family Circle, if you make that claim.

An assignment is a business arrangement in which the
editor employs you to write an article. Clips beget assignments.
That's a basic fact of the writing life. The more clips you have
and the better they are, the better the jobs you will land. This
becomes a continual process of building credit on credit. The
writing credits you build up are the only things that move you
up in the profession. Moving up means a better reputation, a
better reputation means better writing jobs, and better jobs
mean more money. So in the cycle of your work, clips are key
to your growth and success as a magazine writer.

Now that you know you need clips to grow your career,
what happens if you're just starting out and don't have them?
Are there ways to come up with something before your magazine writing career is really going? There are three.

First, look for opportunities where certain small items
are solicited right in the pages of a magazine. You've read them,
boxed off at the end of an article. "Tell us your story in 250
words, and if we publish it we'll pay you $50." The competi-
tion is stiff for these shorties, but on the bright side, the competition consists of everyone who reads the magazine, not
just other writers. As a writer, you should have an advantage
here. Find ten to twenty of these little gems, then write and

send them in, every month. In fact, send as many as you can as often as you can. Persistence pays off at any level of your career, and these solicited items are a great way to train yourself in the fine art of persistence.

When you've had a few successes and a few paychecks, photocopy your successes onto a single page. Four or five pieces arranged on one page look better than one tiny article sitting alone in the middle of a big white page. Then attach it to your query as a clip. Make sure, however, that you let the editor know this is only the beginning of your career. While these shorties are not considered heavy hitters in the clip world, they do show an editor that you are persistent and serious about writing. And they boast just a bit of your writing style. They can also lead to a small assignment, such as a filler.

Second, don't overlook your local newspaper as a source for spearing your first clip. Most newspapers rely on stringers as sources of articles other than what are assigned to regular staff writers. In large newspapers, stringer articles are typically human-interest stories and local happenings that are not considered hard news. In small papers, they can be local news, as well as stories with a human-interest angle.

A newspaper has no obligation to buy a stringer's stories, but a stringer who produces good work consistently can usually find a place in print. Unfortunately, stringer articles are notoriously poor payers, and some small newspapers don't pay for them at all. When you write a freebie, though, as most freelancers do at some point in their career, keep in mind that the value of the clip it will produce will offset the lack of a paycheck and will pay off many times over in the future. Poor pay aside, the good news about gathering stringer clips is that while magazines take months to publish your work, you could have a newspaper clip in hand, with your byline at the top, within just a few days.

Third, as mentioned in Chapter 3, write as an expert. Expert credentials look good with clips, but they can stand alone, without clips, as well. When you pitch the story, emphasize your expertise and explain why it makes you the perfect one to write the article.

What Clips to Send

After your clips start rolling in, you'll have to decide which ones to send with your query letter. Of course, send your best. At first, you may not have much from which to select, but send what you have. If you've had only one article published, send the first page from it. If you've had two, send the first page from each. But once you've had several articles published, start to customize the clips you send. Send a clip from a home-decorating article when you are querying to write another article on home decorating. If you are querying a magazine that has published you before, send a clip of that article to let its editors know they trusted you once and that trust paid off.

To compile your clips package, choose three or four good ones, then photocopy the first page from each, filling no more than two sheets of paper, front and back. Don't send more than four clips and don't send an entire article, because editors don't have time to read them.

Occasionally you'll run across a magazine that requests tearsheets. A tearsheet is the actual article, torn from the magazine. Years ago, magazines customarily sent their writers dozens of tearsheets to use as clips. This is not a common practice today, so when you see the word *tearsheet,* don't worry about sending one, just send a photocopy instead. A good example of your published work is what counts, not whether it's being submitted as a tearsheet or as a photocopy.

Two last tips on clips. Send them only if they are neat and clean. Clips that have gone out more than one time look like it, so throw them away and start over. Avoid using colored paper, too. It's hard on an editor's tired eyes.

The Query Letter

Writing the letter that will either get or lose you an assignment can be a little daunting. You already know that your query must be focused, brief, and professional, but how can you accomplish this, sell your idea, and prove that you are the best writer for the job, all in the confines of just a few short paragraphs?

It's tough, there's no getting around it; but thousands of magazine writers are doing it successfully every day. Of course, thousands more are doing it unsuccessfully, too. How you write and present your query will determine the thousands of writers with whom you'll stand.

The query letter comes out of the simple process of asking for work, and there are no absolutes in writing it. What works for one writer may not work for another, so if you attend a workshop where someone tells you there is only one way to compose a good query, don't believe it; it's not true. Every writer develops a personal style and preference. Every writer's query letter also evolves over the course of a career. The first query you ever wrote will not be like the one you will write five years down the line, because you will grow in experience and in your personal expression and writing style.

As discussed earlier in this chapter, professionally phrased queries are usually best, and informal queries do not generally work until you have developed a personal relationship with your editor. But if you have a killer informal style that works, go with it. If you don't have a refined style yet, whether informal or professional, stick to something easy. A basic four-paragraph letter can tell your editor everything he needs to know.

Paragraph One

The purpose of this paragraph is, in a few short sentences, to demonstrate a need for this article. Use a personal anecdote, or draw conclusions from personal observations. For example:

> Sixty-four ounces a day is a lot to swallow, but the benefits outweigh the inconvenience. We all know we should drink water, we've all heard there are health and nutrition benefits, but beyond that we don't give the water we drink much thought. In fact, we take it for granted. It's always there when you turn on the tap, or open the refrigerator. And when you go to the gym, have you noticed how many of those little bottles are always lying around?

Another example, written from the personal perspective, works equally well:

> Collecting is one of the fundamental joys of childhood. I still have my dolls and, grudgingly, at age 35, I turned over my rock collection to my daughter. As for my seashells—the memories of collecting them, with my parents, are far too precious for me to get rid of the shells, even though I don't really have room to keep them.

Either opening paragraph grabs the editor's attention, tells him what's coming, and gives him a chance to focus on the subject you are about to propose.

Paragraph Two

This paragraph is where you make the hard sell. You tell the editor what you will write, how you will write it, and what you will include in the body of the article. Facts, statistics, basic research, and anything that transforms your article from something off the top of your head into something that shows planning are all elements that work in this section. Offer experts' quotes, sidebars, and photos in this paragraph too. (More about this in the next section.) For example:

> I would like to write an article about the water we drink, including
>
> - Why the body needs it/nutritional requirements and health benefits.
> - Types of water available: tap, well, artesian, mineral, sparkling, spring, distilled.
> - Why people are choosing bottled water.
> - Tap water versus bottled water/what's in the tap water we drink.

- Water filters for tap water.
- Sidebar on the history of bottled water, including George Washington's connection.
- Resource sidebar including free information on brands of approved bottled water.
- Sidebar on how to find out if your tap water is safe.
- Interviews with a public health expert, a nutritionist, and a water industry expert.

This paragraph is loaded with basic facts that tell the editor there is enough information available to go forward with an entire article on water. The editor who bought the water article wrote in her acceptance letter that "I read over your water query and I must say, I like it very much. It appears that you plan to address all of the angles. Do you know how uncommon it is to find a writer who tackles a project in this way?"

Consider another example, again from a personal perspective:

My kids collect. One has a ceramic bird collection she started with her grandmother, another has the rocks we collected as a family when she was young, and the third hoards a whole host of collectibles from baseball cards to fossils. And yes, we have a cluttered house, but the clutter is something we've accumulated, and cherish, as a family. The childhood collections we have pursued strengthen our family relationships, holding us together when a lot of things in a house full of teenagers pull us apart, and this is the story I would like to write. Through my family's experiences this article, with the working title "From Rocks to Teddy Bears: A Family's Joy of Childhood Collecting," will

- Tell why collecting is important in the family relationship.
- Explain why children collect.
- Tell how the family can turn collecting into something fun for everyone.
- Guide parents in helping their children start and maintain a collection.
- Discuss why the actual collecting, and not what's collected, is what's important.
- Talk about family traditions that could stem from collecting.

Again, both queries take a different form to discuss what the article will include, but both let the editor know exactly what to expect.

Paragraph Three

If you are firmly convinced that your clips will speak for themselves, continue the pitch in this paragraph. If not, blow your horn here. Tell where you've been published, include a list of professional credits that will lend themselves to the article, and use anything that will convince the editor you can do the job. Also mention that you are enclosing clips, so that if your letter becomes separated from your clips and the editor likes what he sees in the query, he will know to look for or request another set of clips. This paragraph should be short, no more than four or five sentences. For example:

> I know this query seems dry. Most of my queries do. But my writing style is much lighter, as you can tell from the clips I've enclosed. To add a note to my credentials, I was a critical-care nurse prior to becoming a writer, which gives me the medical knowledge necessary to write this article.

Or:

> Enclosed is a clip of my last article published in your magazine. The style of the article I'm proposing would be very similar.

Or:

> Samples of my writing are enclosed. My other writing credits include...

You don't need to go into great depth at this point, because too much depth gets wordy, and using too many words will in fact cut words from the most important part of your query letter—the pitch. But do offer your editor enough information to give him a sense of the writer he will be hiring if you are using this paragraph to highlight your credits. If you are using it to continue your pitch, add more details. For example:

> An interesting debate concerning bottled water is the fluoride issue. Are we lacking fluoride because we drink bottled water, and if so, what are the consequences? Or, perhaps, are we getting enough fluoride from other sources, such as toothpaste, mouth rinses, and foods that are prepared and packed in water? This article will include the results of the latest research in this debate and offer expert advice from one of the nation's leading oral biologists.

Paragraph Four

This section is a mini-pitch, to emphasize what you said in paragraph two, but in a different way. It also thanks the editor for his time. Don't include phrases such as "I hope you'll like my story" or "I really would like to work for you." It weakens an otherwise strong query and shows the editor that you are not as confident about your work as you should be. Always assume that you will get the job, write your query letter accordingly, and tell the editor you look forward to hearing from him. For example:

> A 19th-century ad claimed that bottled water was "emetic, cathartic, and diuretic; good in scrofulous and rheumatic affectations, likewise in venereal taints...." I don't know about those claims, but I do know that the most healthful drink known to man is back in the limelight. Everyone drinks it in some form, and I believe your readers will benefit from knowing more about what they are drinking. I appreciate your consideration, and look forward to hearing from you.

Likewise:

> My son's fossil collection is a killer, and when he shows it to friends the story of when and how he found each and every fossil is as important as his explanation of what the fossil is. We plan family excursions around fossil hunting, which create memories that will outlive my son's desire to collect and my husband's and my ability to go on the hunt. This is what collecting is all about, though—the time together, and the memories—and this is the story I'd like to tell your readers. I appreciate your consideration, and look forward to hearing from you.

Your own query may be vastly different in style from anything you've read here or elsewhere, but the basic elements are always the same. These four surefire components are big winners, no matter how you write them:

1. An opener that catches the editor's attention.
2. The pitch.

3. Why you're the one for the job.
4. A thank you.

Now let's return to paragraph two, to discuss experts, sidebars, and photos. A combination of at least two of these elements is something every editor wants to see offered in a query.

Experts

Finding an expert frightens most beginners, as well as many seasoned veterans. The process is cloaked in a veil of mystery. Writers who are successful at lining up the best experts won't tell how they do it, because a good expert is a valuable commodity. But finding an expert is not such a difficult task. Admittedly, it does take nerves to call someone out of the blue and ask him to tell you everything he knows about a certain subject. Because most people love to see their name in print, however, the task becomes easier. So let's look at the three basic factors involved in adding an expert's advice to your article.

First, who is an expert? Unless you are presenting yourself as the expert for the piece, an expert is anyone who isn't you. It's a friend, someone you met at a meeting, or someone you heard speak somewhere. It's your doctor, your minister, your lawyer, or your mother's doctor, minister, or lawyer. Your dog's vet is an expert, as is your child's kindergarten teacher. The world is full of experts.

Next, how do you get an expert? Simply call him up. If you're writing an article on home decorating, check your local yellow pages for an interior decorator. If your article is about bunions, call a podiatrist. Tap experts in your own area if you are writing for a local publication, but if you are pitching this for a national publication it's best to find your experts in a broader geographic area. Normally, one from any given state is all an editor wants to see. Check your library for telephone directories of different cities around the country, and call as you would in your own area.

Seek out different associations, foundations, and organizations for experts too. For example, if you intend to write an article about some aspect of arthritis, check your phone book for the Arthritis Foundation, then call and ask local representatives for a referral to someone on the national level. While you are thinking about experts, university professors can be experts on every imaginable subject. If you are writing an article on how to give a speech, call a university and ask to speak to someone who teaches speech courses.

You don't want too many, or too few, experts for your article. Too many clutter it and make it look like a laundry list of quotes and citations. Too few will seem to bias your article toward one point of view or opinion. Generally, using one expert for about every 500 words you write is sufficient. This ratio gives you a good blend of story and expertise.

Many magazine editors will ask for an anecdote or two, to add a human-interest angle to your story. Anecdotes are much more difficult to find, because there are no lists of them in library books and you cannot find them in the yellow pages, but don't worry. There are three ways to find someone with just the right personal story for your article. First, use your own story. Many writers do this, which works well. Second, ask friends. You could be amazed by what goes on in their lives. Third, ask your expert. When someone is considered an expert on a subject, he will certainly know someone who has a personal story. Your interior designer probably has a satisfied client who would be thrilled to tell her story. Your podiatrist may well have a patient who would love to relate his tale of foot care.

Finally, the most difficult part of your quest for an expert is making the actual approach. The encouraging news is that you don't have to do it in person. In-person interviews are rarely expected of freelance magazine writers, because most magazines won't pick up the travel tab for freelancers. They should pay telephone costs, however, which spares you the ordeal of a face-to-face interview. Of course, an in-person interview with a local expert is always a good way to sharpen your own interpersonal communication skills.

For a telephone interview, follow these steps:

- Explain who you are, the subject of your article, the magazine for which you are writing, and how long the interview should take. Normally, you should be able to complete an interview in less than half an hour.

- Ask to set up an appointment for this interview. You wouldn't just barge into someone's office expecting to hold an interview on the spot, and phone interviews are no different. Some experts will be ready right then, however, so don't call unprepared. Be ready to conduct your interview the first time you make the approach. And always allow for differences in time zones.

- When you set the appointment, talk about the specific topic you want your expert to address. For instance, instead of just asking her to talk about water, ask her about the purity of bottled water compared to tap water.

- Take good notes. Tape recording is also acceptable, but make sure you get permission, on tape, before you do. Take notes even when you tape an interview, because a broken tape or other mechanical difficulties can happen, leaving you without an interview if you haven't backed it up in writing.

- Start with your expert's name, verifying its spelling and her credentials. Then ask your questions.

- Be flexible. An expert can lead you in a direction you did not anticipate, but if that direction is useful to your article, go with it. However, when an expert wanders off the topic, wait for a pause in the conversation, then lead back to it with your next question.

- Make the phone call on your dime. Don't call collect, and don't lure an expert into an interview if she returns your call. Ask to hang up and call her right back. If you have a contract for this assignment, make sure it includes a clause for reimbursement of phone expenses. If it doesn't, write it in and ask your editor to okay it. If you are writing without a contract, phone expenses will probably come out of your pocket.

- Tell your expert that you will send her a copy of the article when it is published. If you are not writing an article assigned by an editor but one that you hope to sell (called writing on speculation), tell your expert.

It's not fair to let her think her words are about to be published when you can't be sure they will be.

When you interview in person, follow all these guidelines, plus dress professionally and be on time. If you have to cancel or postpone an interview for some reason, let your expert know as far in advance as possible.

Sidebars

Experts are easy to find, sidebars easy to create. Go grab your favorite magazine and turn to a feature article. Do you see a little box of related information stuck in the middle, along the side, or at the bottom of almost every page? That's a sidebar. It's information that parallels your story but doesn't quite fit into it. If you're writing about the health benefits of bottled water, include a sidebar telling how George Washington tried to buy into the nation's leading mineral water bottler of the day. Sidebars can also highlight one particular aspect of your story, offer resources for readers to consult for more information, or be a quiz like those commonly found in women's magazines.

A sidebar breaks up the visual monotony of a written page, and editors love them. Offer at least two for a 1500-word article, more if you have the ideas. Their word count can be anywhere from 50 to 300 words. Most editors are flexible about the sidebars they accept, so be creative. Find some related books your readers might like to know about, or a brochure they can send away for. If you are writing about dry skin, for example, draft a little quiz that will tell your readers if they have a problem. Does your skin itch? Are you plagued by unsightly red patches? Six to ten questions will usually work, and they don't need to be scientific—just informative—with their answers found in the body of the article.

Photographs

You can offer photos even if you're not a professional photographer. First check magazines' guidelines to see if they want photos. Many do, but some do not. The standard format is 35 millimeter, with magazines accepting black and whites or color prints or transparencies (slides). If you are an amateur, offer only these basics. If you don't know which camera button to press, don't offer. If you are a professional, though, give them everything you have. Good photos will sell an article.

When you shoot photos or slides, type up a simple form including your name, the subject's name, and a statement granting you permission to use the photo in print. This form, called a model release, grants the photographer permission to use the photo and absolves him from liability if the final published product is blurry or distorted, which is not your fault. Following is a basic example of a release. If you are shooting photos of a house or in a store or other privately owned building or facility, get permission to publish these photos too. Change the release to reflect what you are shooting.

Model Release

I (model's name) grant (photographer's name) permission to publish photographs of me taken at (place) on (date). (Photographer) will not be held responsible for image blurring, distortion, or alteration in the finished product, unless the aforementioned is proven to be done purposely, with malicious intent toward me.

I also grant permission for these images to be published in any print manner, including periodicals and newspapers.

Model's Name_____

Address_____

City, State, Zip_____

Phone_____

Model's Signature _____ Date_____

Photographer's Signature _____ Date_____

Parent/guardian name
   (if model is under 18)_____ Date_____

Enclose a caption for each photo, identifying what it is and who is in it. Don't worry if your picture looks a little crooked or you snapped something in the background that shouldn't be there. Magazine photography departments can work miracles from very little.

The Neat Package

A great query letter offering everything an editor wants to see is a good start in securing the writing assignment you want, but it isn't enough by itself. You need a professional package surrounding that letter, too, one that makes your work stand out. A neat package is simple, putting it together takes little effort, and it can make the difference between having your query accepted or rejected. Your neat package should include:

1. *Good-quality paper, such as linen.* Used for your query or cover letter, it makes a good first impression and is worth the extra cost. Everything else you send can be on less expensive paper. White and off-white are the best colors for your query.
2. *Basic, legible printer fonts.* Easy to read fonts are much more apt to be read by an editor than something fancy.
3. *Standard business letter form,* with a simple letterhead at the top of your page. Your letterhead doesn't have to be something from a professional printer. Create it on your computer or typewriter, including your name, address, phone and fax numbers, and e-mail address.

    Justify the body of your letter to the left, single space the lines, and block and separate each paragraph, instead of indenting them. Here's a useful format to follow.

JJ DeSpain

Street Address ~ City, State ~ Zip Code
Tel: (000)000-0000 ~ Fax:(000)000-0000
E-mail: 000@000.com

Date

Editor's name
Magazine's name (in italics or all caps)
Street address
City, State, Zip Code

Dear Ms., Mr., or Mrs.

Paragraph One (following suggested guidelines above)

Paragraph Two

Paragraph Three

Paragraph Four

Sincerely,

Your Name

Experiment with your letterhead format and the exact style you wish to use as much as you want to, so long as your letter is neat, its spelling accurate, and its grammar and punctuation correct. These are the things editors are trained to look for.

4. *Business cards.* They are cheap, and they look nice attached to your letter. If an editor likes what he sees, he may file your card away for future reference.

5. *A self-addressed stamped envelope (SASE)* must accompany every query. Most editors will not use their own envelopes or postage to return a response to your query, so if you want a response, send a SASE. When you mail outside the United States, domestic postage cannot be

used for a return response. In other words, your U.S.
stamp will take your letter anywhere in the world, but
the same one cannot be used to send mail from anywhere in the world back to you. To receive a response
from outside the country, purchase an international
reply coupon (IRC) to send with your addressed return
envelope instead of a stamp. It is redeemable in most
countries for postage. IRCs can be purchased at the post
office, but they are not always available, so call ahead. Be
prepared for the cost, too, which is more than three
times the normal postal rate.

6. *Clean copies.* They let an editor think he or she is
   the first person to lay hands on your query.
7. *Paper clip the items in your package;* do not staple
   them. Editors like to pull everything apart and spread
   it out. Your business card goes on top, followed by
   your query letter, then the SASE and the clips.
8. *A 9 × 12 envelope.* This beats folding and jamming
   everything into a #10, legal-sized envelope. A 9 × 12
   is larger than everything going across the editor's
   desk. Editors will appreciate not having to straighten
   out folded papers, and larger envelopes will stand out
   in the pile. Just a plain one will do, though. Don't go
   with something like neon pink. You want to be noticed, not laughed at.
9. *Proper postage.* A 9 × 12 automatically bumps you
   up to the next postage rate, and depending upon how
   many papers you include in your package, you could
   move yourself up yet another notch. If you are in
   doubt, have the envelope weighed at the post office,
   or buy a postage scale to weigh it yourself.

Editors read queries every day, and after a while all queries begin to look alike. Follow these simple instructions and
your query will stand out as professional in a pile that smacks
of ordinary.

Electronic Queries

Electronic queries, or e-queries, are relatively new to the magazine industry and are not widely accepted yet. Some magazines welcome and even solicit e-queries, but many don't, so make sure the magazine you intend to approach will accept the e-query you are about to send. If you can't find this in the guidelines, give the magazine a call.

The standard four-paragraph format discussed earlier also works for an electronic submission. The only difference is that you cannot send clips easily, so in the paragraph explaining your credentials, you need to go into more depth. You can scan your clips into your e-mail as an attachment, but in this day of computer viruses it's unlikely than an editor will download anything from a stranger. So ask the editor if he would like you to forward your clips by mail or fax.

Don't assume that when you query an electronic magazine you can do it electronically. These magazines are the new kids on the block, their pay rates are competitive, and they are seeking the best writers with the best experience. To find a legitimate place in the magazine market, many do not accept electronic queries, because they want to see the whole package from a prospective writer. So again, ask first before you query, remembering that the purpose of the query process is to let the editor see the best you've got. If you can do this electronically, it saves the hassle and expense of compiling a complete query package. But if you can't, or if you're not sure you can sell your writing without the solid professional image of a good query package, stick to that.

Selling on Speculation

You've no doubt seen the movie in which a writer has a flash of inspiration and then just sits down, writes a story, and sends it off to a magazine. Now that you've learned about the importance of a good query letter, the first question that should come to mind is, "Did she send a query first?" The answer is, probably not. Unless you've read a few how-to books on getting published or have attended a writing seminar, you won't have a clue about the query process.

What this writer has done, and what many others do, is write a story and send it in on speculation, or spec. By writing on spec you assume the risk of writing the story and sending it to an editor, without knowing if he is interested in your topic or your writing style. Many writers and lecturers will tell you not to submit on spec, which is probably good advice, because otherwise you may put a lot of time and effort into something that will not result in being published. Writing without a contract is chancy, considering that the odds are against your making a sale. If you are a new writer, however, and you don't have clips or a vast résumé of experience, writing on spec may be the only way an editor will ever see your work. The goal of every writer should of course be to get an editor to see her work.

Writing on spec is instrinsically neither good nor bad. Sometimes, as noted, it's a necessity to jump start a career, but often it's a waste of time. Some editors will accept spec manuscripts, even though they do not solicit them, but many will not look at, or accept, spec work in any shape or form. Still, hundreds of magazines do request that articles be sent on spec. This is so usually because they do not want to become involved in the contract process before they've had a look at the final product. A contract obligates them to some form of payment and a publishing commitment, so if an editor has not worked with the writer before and thus does not know how the writer's work will turn out, offering a contract can be risky, especially for little magazines with small editorial budgets.

If you decide to take the plunge by avoiding the query route and going straight to writing, make sure the magazine you wish to approach will indeed accept an article on speculation. If so, follow the same general guidelines for the speculation package that you would for a good query package. Write a cover letter on good-quality paper, explaining a little about the article and yourself. Enclose clips if you have them, plus a business card and a

SASE. Put all this in a 9 × 12 envelope. The professional approach is just as important in selling an actual story as in selling an idea in a query letter.

When and How Often to Query

Lead time is the time it takes from when your article is accepted to when it is published. Lead times vary a good deal. You may be lucky and see your article in print within a few months, but you could wait for well over a year. The available space, similar topics, and the number of articles in line in front of yours are just a few of the editorial factors that will determine when your article will appear. Because you cannot control the factors that determine lead time, it is best to query with general topics all through the year. If you wish to send a seasonal story, however, don't wait until September or October, when the holiday spirit hits you, to submit a Christmas story or query. Most seasonal and holiday pieces are in the final stages of editorial development at least nine months prior to publication, so submit that Christmas story in January and the Halloween query in November.

How Many Queries?

There is no magic formula about how many queries you should send every week or month. The decision is up to you, but you should realize that to make a living as a freelance magazine writer you must keep looking for work. This is a never-ending process, because the work won't come to you. Considering that the odds are nine to one against your query being accepted, if you send out only one or two each week or month it could take months or even years to receive a first acceptance. When you send out ten queries each week or month, you improve your odds. Sending out fifty or sixty might have you looking at your first byline in no time at all.

A question all new writers ask is, Can I send multiple queries? In other words, can a writer send the same, or a similar, query to several different magazines at the same time?

The answer is both yes and no. Many diligent freelancers find a great idea and send it to five or six magazines at the same time to expedite the process. Because response times to queries vary from a couple of weeks to a few months, and in some cases run much longer, sending a multiple query can in fact save time. For the freelancer who wants to make a living selling articles, this is important. Time is money, and you cannot afford to await an answer for weeks or months, only to receive a rejection, then be faced with starting over again. So many freelancers send multiple queries.

The disadvantage of multiple queries comes when more than one editor shows some interest in buying your article and you have to explain that you are also negotiating with another magazine. Most editors will not need or want to negotiate, because they have stacks of queries from other writers waiting for their break. So you may have to inform an editor that your article is no longer available if you have received another offer or made another deal.

Like everything else in writing, the choice of sending out multiple queries is strictly up to you. If it works and you feel comfortable, do it. But if it makes you a little nervous, wondering what you might have to do when two magazines want the same story, you would probably do well to avoid the situation until you have more experience dealing with editors.

Consider a few more tips about sending out multiple queries. Unless otherwise noted in their guidelines, magazine editors expect, and accept, them. They will not hold it against you if you have already made a deal for an article they might have wanted, because they know how tough it is to get work. And, since they liked your work once, you stand a better shot of having them take a serious look the next time you send something.

Sending out multiple completed manuscripts on speculation is a different story, however. An editor with your good manuscript in hand is less likely to be forgiving when you tell him you've already sold it to someone else. Unless the magazine's guidelines specifically state that simultaneous submissions are welcome, don't send them. When you do send simultaneous submissions, note in your cover letter that you have done so.

A Few More Query Tips

Volumes have been written on the query letter, often making it seem the most daunting part of writing. The query is important, and even if you choose to write on speculation you will need to develop a good query style, because most editors prefer to be approached by a query rather than be bombarded by unsolicited manuscripts. In other words, to succeed in the magazines you've got to master the query. So consider everything you've read in this chapter, keep what you think will work for you and discard the rest, then look at a last few tips.

1. Query the same editor over and over, even if that person has earlier rejected you. Editors do remember names, and once yours becomes recognized and your query stands out as better than most, your name may go into a file marked "potential."
2. If an editor rejects a query, send it back nine to twelve months later. Editors read so many submissions, they likely won't remember one they saw months ago, and often what was not right the first time may just hit the spot later on.
3. Customize each query. A standard, basic form works from magazine to magazine, but include the magazine's name once or twice in the body of the query and throw in the editor's name wherever you can, apart from the address and greeting at the top of the page. Make sure all your editor and magazine names match before you send out the letter.
4. Keep track of your queries. Compose a simple log that will track each submission, and use it to refresh your memory about the editors and magazines you are querying.

Submission Tracking Sheet

Magazine name/address_____

Editor's name_____ Date submitted_____

What submitted (query, spec article, assigned
     article)_____

Multiple submission? Yes__ No__

Previously submitted to other magazines? Yes__
     No__ Where_____ When_____

Date accepted_____ Publication date_____
     Deadline_____

Payment_____ Payment due date_____
     Rights sold_____

Contract, letter of agreement,
     verbal agreement_____

Date rejected_____
     Personal or form rejection_____

Comments and article instructions:

Don't Go Too Far

One of the most unfortunate situations that happens to all
magazine writers is that they offer an editor a good query, it is
rejected, and half a year later the article appears, written by
someone else. Sometimes it's a coincidence, but at other times
it's a case of an editor's passing the original query along to one
of his regular writers.

When this happens, there is nothing you can do about it
except grit your teeth and vow never to send another query
to that editor. To prevent such a situation, include enough
information in your query letter to make your idea sound
appealing, but not enough that someone else can take your
outline, call your experts, and write an easy story.

One editor with a family-issues magazine had a habit of
sending the best queries she received to her best friend, then
rejecting the writer who had initially offered them. She particularly loved the queries that came with full details: the

source of information, experts' names, and contact information. She even went so far as to lead writers on, telling them the article was promising but she needed more information to make the final decision.

This is fortunately a rare occurrence, but any magazine writer with even a moderate amount of experience has probably had it happen more than once. To prevent it, hold back the specific details until you have a contract.

1. Never reveal your expert's name until you have a contract. Most editors will be satisfied to know you will be interviewing a genetic engineer for your cloning article without knowing your expert's name.
2. When you present statistics or facts in your query, do not cite the sources.
3. If your editor insists on details you do not want to give, explain your reasons. If he still insists on having that expert's name and phone number before he will offer a contract, be wary!

Query on, query often, and query well. If you want to be a freelance magazine writer who finds paychecks in the mail, think of the query as your best friend, because it is. The magazine industry moves forward on the merit of your query, and while many editors consider them a necessary evil, queries do provide the skeleton of what goes into every issue. Years ago, magazines employed regular writers to fill their pages, and the query was not a vital ingredient in the mix. Today magazines employ very few regular writers and their editors rely heavily on freelance work. So even though the editors may gripe, their brightest and best work comes from the pile of necessary evils stacked on their desks. But what they take from the stack and ultimately publish has to be the best of the bunch or it gets demoted to the stack marked "unnecessary evil."

5

After You've Sent It In

He that can have patience, can have what he will.
—Benjamin Franklin

IT CERTAINLY takes patience for the next step of the process, because the first thing you have to do at this stage is wait. Whether you've sent in a complete manuscript or a query, you now wait for an acceptance or a rejection. You wait for the contract to arrive. You wait while your editor decides exactly how your article is to be written and rewritten. For whatever reason, you wait, and while waiting isn't easy, it is vital to your success as a magazine writer. So if you're not good at waiting, practice.

The toughest wait comes from the moment you drop your query into the mailbox until you receive a response. The length of time it takes to receive a response varies, from a week or two to as long as a year. Some editors read queries and manuscripts sent on spec once a day, some once a week. Some may pile them up for a month or two, but others may never read them at all, passing the chore off to an editorial assistant. Another sad reality is that some submissions are rejected out

of hand as they arrive, before they are read. You may even receive no response at all, even when you've done everything right,
including sending a SASE. Receiving no response is an ever-grow-
ing trend in the magazine market, because many editors assume
that no response equals an implied rejection. For you, unfortunately, no response is a waste of time and money.

No matter what sort of response you receive (or don't) never
take it personally. It's not a personal slam against you. Just
because an editor fails to respond to a query it took you six
hours to put together, or to that spec manuscript it took you a
month to write, it doesn't mean that she has it in for you. It just
suggests that at the moment these submissions are not high on
her priority list. It means that she has every article she needs
for the next nine months under contract already. It means that
your query was lost in the mail. It means that your spec manuscript fell behind the editor's file cabinet.

There is no rhyme or reason for the way many queries
and unsolicited manuscripts are treated, but unless you've
made yourself a particular nuisance to an editor and that
editor's hands begin to shake when she sees your name, don't
worry. You'll get responses the way every magazine freelancer
does. Some will be good, many bad, and a few will never come.
It's merely part of the job, so be patient.

Rejection

One thing all writers have in common is an aversion to the "r"
word, rejection. Nothing unites writers of poetry, nonfiction, and
fiction so much as that nasty piece of paper slipped into the mailbox after weeks of waiting for an editor's response.

Unfortunately, to be a writer is to be rejected. Rejection
is a way of life, a record of your efforts, and a great way to
thicken your skin.

You may have met the writer who is so deadly afraid of
being rejected that he fills his closet with manuscripts, careful
never to let an editor take a peek at them for fear of being
zapped with the big "r." Then there is the writer who tucks
away the rejection as it arrives, tells no one about it, and has a
nervous breakdown. This writer may actually hold the returned

envelope up to the light, see that there is a form rejection inside, and throw it away without ever opening it. Some writers claim to paper their walls with rejections; others simply discard them. A wise writer, however, will learn from the rejections. There are in fact lessons to be learned that let you know how close you are to being published, whether your submission has even been read, and what the editor thinks of your writing.

When your work is rejected, you can expect to receive one of five responses. First, form rejections are the most expedient way for an editor to dispatch a submission. It's usually a third- or fourth-generation photocopy, starting with "Dear Writer," followed by a thank-you for your effort and a sentence that lets you know your idea does not fit the magazine, and ending by wishing you luck in placing your submission elsewhere. The majority of rejections any beginning writer receives are form letters. If you receive one within a week of submitting a query or spec manuscript, chances are your work was not read. If a form rejection arrives after two weeks, your submission has probably received fair consideration. But don't be surprised to have a few year-old rejections trickle in. One writer of children's articles actually received a rejection eight years after submitting a story.

The second form of rejection is a handwritten note tacked on the bottom of a form rejection, especially when you are beginning to make an impression in the publishing world. Your work has been recognized and an editor has taken the time to offer encouragement, even if it is in the form of a rejection with a few personal words scrawled across the bottom. This professional courtesy means that you are getting closer to being published. The more personal the rejection, the more seriously your work is being considered. So submit another piece to this editor within two weeks, including a thank-you for the previous consideration, and mention the note you received. Never put off an opportunity such as that of responding to a personally written note, because personal contact in any form can be the beginning of a publishing relationship.

The third kind of rejection, the personal one, shows a definite interest by the editor. An editor who takes the time to offer a personal response has seen merit in your work, even if it does not fit the needs of that publishing house at the time. You are being considered a serious, professional writer worthy of being published, but you happen to have offered an idea that is not suitable at present. The journey from form rejection to personal rejection is a yardstick of accomplishment, because it measures where you have been and where you are about to go. As with the form rejection endorsed with a handwritten note, submit another of your works to this editor as soon as you can.

The fourth kind of rejection, an invitation to submit something else, can happen in a rejection letter, either at the bottom of a form rejection or in a personal one. You may receive a note indicating that the editor would like to see another example of your work. When you send it, include a copy of the letter with the invitation, just to jog the editor's memory. Again, submit it as quickly as possible. Strike while the iron is hot, nothing being hotter than an invitation to submit your work.

The final form of rejection can result in an assignment based on something the editor saw in your query or clips, even when the original idea you submitted is being rejected. The editor may like your writing style and your clips but feels that your idea doesn't work. Also, an idea that doesn't work for the magazine may still strike up an idea in your editor for an article on a similar topic. For example, you might submit a query on how children react to pain from scrapes and cuts, at a time when for months the editor has had in the back of her mind a piece on getting stitches. She sees your query and decides that you can write the piece she really wants. This happens all the time.

Good and Bad Rejection Advice

When it comes to submissions and rejections, a lot of bad advice is circulating. You may read it in writing magazines or hear it at conferences. In the end, however, it's up to you to decide what is best for your writing career. But consider using the following good tips before you come to any conclusions.

Always include a SASE. The two worst pieces of information you will hear pertain to SASEs. The first is not to include a SASE, because if your work is accepted you will be notified by phone. This is not always the case. Many assignments and contracts will come back in your SASE. The second piece of bad information deals with making the editor's job easier by including a postcard typed with the words *accepted* or *rejected* for the editor to mark off and return. This is terrible advice. As we have just seen, any rejection you receive can be packed full of information vital to advancing your writing career, so if you include a return postcard limiting the editor to two choices you will probably receive nothing more than a checkmark, which will tell you nothing. But let the editor send a rejection and maybe you'll receive that handwritten note or invitation to submit something else.

Keep your rejections. Experts will tell you that they can be valuable at tax time as proof of your work, which is true if you decide to claim your writing as a legitimate job. Granted, no one likes receiving rejections. You'd probably prefer to throw them in the trash when they arrive, but don't. Instead, set up a special file in which to toss all rejection letters. One that looks suspiciously like a trash can can have an amazingly cathartic effect, but make sure you don't accidentally empty it with the real trash.

Resubmit your material. Most good manuscripts and ideas will eventually find a home. You may find that some of your work will be accepted by the same publisher who initially rejected it. Much of it will probably find its home with other publishers, however. There are countless opportunities for writers who don't back down from a rejection. Good writing and strong ideas will get published. They may be rejected initially, but these rejections do not have to be the final word unless you accept a rejection as a finality.

A few last thoughts on rejections. Think of them as a challenge to improve upon your idea, to target a better-suited publisher for your work, to update or revise your query or spec manuscript package, or to establish a relationship with a new editor. Rejections may be the end of your work, or they can be what it takes to open new doors. But you do have to be realistic. There will come a time when you've had so many rejections that putting your query aside for something new will be the wise choice. If it's a project that you're convinced should be published, put it away for a year, then dust it off and try again. Don't kid yourself, though. This piece could then face rejection again. Or it could be bought by an editor who has already turned it down twice. Just remember that how you succeed as a magazine writer will be determined by what you learn from your rejections.

The Article Proposal

You may find yourself at a point when your query looks good and your editor may be showing an interest in your project, but she's still undecided about you: Are you up to the task, is your writing really good enough to pull off the entire project, and can she trust you to meet the deadline? Whatever the case, you are halfway through the door, but your editor needs a little extra reassurance to bring you all the way in. Usually, at this stage of the process she may ask you to do one of two things—write the article on speculation, or develop a more detailed outline or proposal.

Both suggestions place the burden on you to produce work, without a guarantee that you will be paid for your efforts. If under normal circumstances you never write a spec manuscript, don't start now. Let your editor know that you are not comfortable about taking the risk without any guarantees, and ask if she would consider a compromise: one completed page of manuscript plus a sidebar or any other small portion that will show what you can do. This compromise could also come in the form of a proposal, but again you would be doing the work without a commitment from your editor.

A proposal is a detailed outline of what an article will contain. It breaks the article into logical sections, includes information about the contents of each section, and presents a professional picture of experts and others you will include. In other words, a proposal is a skeleton of the article you intend to write later.

If you have pitched an article without considering how you intend to construct it, writing a proposal could take a lot of work. If, however, in your background research you've already put together an overview of the article for your own benefit, expanding it into a full proposal should not be a problem.

Proposals take time and research, but the good news is that a well-constructed proposal will sell an article to an editor who is already interested, and will make your writing of it easier. It will organize your thoughts and information and lay out the course your article will follow.

Proposal style varies, and how you choose to construct one probably does not matter as much as the information you include. Here are a few examples that work.

Proposal for Vacations for Kids with Disabilities

Dear Editor:

As per your request, I've developed a detailed proposal for a 1,500-word piece (plus sidebar) on accessible vacations for families having kids with disabilities. The body of the article will feature destinations and resources. The sidebar will include tips on how to travel.

I. Experts
1. A professor of childhood development with expertise in family-centered activity and care. She will address the need for family vacations.
2. A professional athlete who has turned his fame into helping disabled kids take skiing lessons. He will address interactive vacations and how sports participation can boost self-esteem.
3. Director of a nonprofit travel organization for children with disabilities.
4. Anecdotes from two families who travel with their disabled children, including comments from their children.

II. Vacation Destinations:
1. I will include all the pertinent accessibility information, what the park or program has to offer the whole family, special arrangements that should be made, costs involved, contact information, etc.
2. I'll list theme parks, several ski schools, a scuba school, and a wilderness adventure program that does everything from backpacking to white-water rafting.
3. Cruises are good vacations for people with disabilities. I'll list a few that are kid friendly. Here I will also mention using travel agencies and include a couple that specialize in travel by the disabled.
5. If there's room, I'd like to list a few good zoos. I've seen some reviews, and maybe a few of the most accessible would work.
III. Resources
Books, Web sites, and magazines specific to disability and travel.
IV. Sidebar
1. Insider travel tips from travelers with disabilities, to parents who are inexperienced in traveling with kids having disabilities
2. Vacations that kids with disabilities can take without their parents—a list of great camps for specific disabilities, plus several integrated camps that take kids with all disabilities.

As you see, this proposal is filled with detail, but not enough to give away all your hard-found information. It is an informal outline, but it contains the information an editor should know to make a final decision.

Another proposal style, more along the lines of an outline, works well, too.

Proposal for Article on Seasonal Affective Disorder (SAD)

I. SAD Overview
   A. Stats
   B. Regional effects (South-to-North increase in incidence)
   C. Breakdown of SAD levels
II. Who Gets SAD
   A. Category breakdown
      1. Family history
      2. Women vs. men
   B. Factors determining diagnosis
      1. Case against self-diagnosis
      2. Similar symptoms, different diagnosis
III. Symptoms
   A. Depression
   B. Lethargy
   C. Carbohydrate craving
   D. Decreased sex drive
IV. Getting Help
   A. What physician to call
      1. Light therapy
      2. Antidepressants
   B. Self-help measures (to assist professional help)
      1. Walk in the sun
      2. Changing the environment (drapes, trees in front of window, etc.)
      3. Diet
      4. Stress factors
      5. Exercise
Experts
Two medical experts, internationally recognized in the field

> 1 light therapy expert
> 1 psychologist specializing in the effects
>   of exercise on depression
> 1 SAD sufferer
> Two Sidebars
>   Resources for more information
>   Summertime SAD

Again, the editor will know what you intend to do from this outline and will have a good idea what to expect if you are offered a contract. How you frame your proposal is a matter of choice. The specifics of the information you include are also up to you. Too little information may cause the editor to think you have not researched your topic well enough. Too much may prove to be a temptation to an editor who is willing to take query ideas from one writer and assign them to another. So in the case of submitting a proposal, it may be best to find the middle ground. Submit enough to prove that you know the topic and can write about it, but not enough that someone else could write it up from your proposal.

Acceptance

Acceptance is the best news you'll get. In this case the editor liked your spec manuscript, or your query is just what he wants. Either you'll get a phone call with the good news or a letter will arrive. Either way, you are suddenly faced with some responsibilities that didn't exist when you were in the early phases of trying to be published. Now establishing an editor's preferred style, the deadline, sidebar requirements, exact word count, method of payment, and rights being bought are important. You have become a writer turned negotiator.

Once you begin the back-and-forth process of negotiating an assignment, do it directly with your editor, either face to face or over the phone. Never negotiate in a letter or fax or by e-mail. As a writer, you know just how easy it is for an editor to reject written words, but in dealing with an actual person rejection becomes more difficult. Also, in a personal negotiation you have an opportunity to respond immediately to the points being raised, good or bad.

Consider these suggestions before you begin negotiating:

1. Take good notes.
2. Listen carefully.
3. Make your point, then be quiet and don't try to fill in the long, silent spaces. This puts your editor in the position of having to respond to you, which is especially good when you are trying to strike a compromise.
4. When the negotiations don't go your way, don't take it out on your editor. She is probably following company policy.
5. Be bold and ask for what you want. The worst you'll hear is *no*, but you may also hear *yes*. Start with small things such as deadlines and word count, then end with payment. Because payment is usually the strongest area of disagreement, don't lead with it or you may alienate your editor for the rest of the process.
6. Be willing to make concessions. Know your priorities, and be ready to give a little to get a little.
7. Negotiate everything at one time, then end the session. Don't go back for more.
8. Get it in writing. This will be the biggest step toward getting what was agreed upon.

Now that you know that the negotiation process is part of the journey on the road to being published, there are some things about which you will need to be very specific in those negotiations.

What Your Editor Wants Is What Your Editor Will Publish

Editors have specific needs, likes, and dislikes, and while a query you sent may be for a 2,000-word essay on summer safety in the backyard, your editor may want 1,200 words, not in essay form but as a bulleted list. Such a list is one of facts, one after the other, with little or no explanation. Here's one example.

Experts from the National Pool and Spa Institute (NPSI) suggest several ways to help make poolside activities safer for your family:

- Use approved personal flotation devices, not inflatable toys.
- Remove toys from the pool area. They attract children to a potentially dangerous area.
- Secure and lock steps and ladders to aboveground pools, or remove them when the pool is not in use.
- Keep a first-aid kit, with telephone and emergency phone numbers handy.
- Secure the entire pool area with a fence four to five feet tall. Fences shouldn't be constructed of vertical bars more than four inches apart or materials like chain link that are easy to climb.
- Gates into the pool area should be self-closing and self-latching, with the latch mounted out of a child's reach. Gate alarms (about $100) can be purchased from pool dealers.
- Remove patio furniture from near pool fences to prevent kids from climbing them.
- Never leave a child unattended even for a minute. If you own a pool, everyone in your family should know how to swim.
- Buy a pool alarm. It sounds when motion is detected in the water. Units with remote receivers that can be placed in areas other than the pool are available from pool dealers for about $150.
- Keep lifesaving equipment poolside, including a ring buoy with an attached line and a long-handled hook.
- Store pool chemicals in a cool, dry, locked cabinet out of children's reach.

Maybe you had visions of writing this part of the article in 700 words and adding much more detail to each suggestion, but this approximately 220-word list is what your editor wants. So, to save yourself time, you should know exactly what you're doing before you start.

Here are five questions you should always ask about any article before you write it.

1. *Style?* Ask your editor if she has copies of other articles written in the style expected from you.
2. *Word count?* Why write 3,000 words if your editor will reject half?
3. *How many sidebars will there be,* and do they apply to the word count? Words go quickly when you are writing, and knowing how you will distribute them is important to your end product.
4. *How many words per sidebar?* Two or three hundred is standard, but some magazines want 50 words, others 500.
5. *Are there any specifics* the editor would like to see, and anything to avoid? An editor's emphasis may be completely different from yours. Your emphasis on backyard safety may be the barbeque grill while hers is the pool.

Getting Paid

Once you are clear about what you are to write and what the editor expects from you, the next step is negotiating the pay. In magazines you'll receive one of several offers. While you may think these are etched in stone, they are not. The payment amount is always open for discussion.

- *Flat fee.* This is a flat price, regardless of the word count.
- *Pay by the column inch.* You'll be offered a certain amount of money based on the number of column inches your piece occupies in print.

- *Pay in copies or a subscription.* No money offered, but you will receive several free copies and possibly a subscription to the magazine for your efforts.
- *Pay by the word.* You will receive anywhere from a few cents to a few dollars per word. This category is a little tricky. You will be paid by the published word, not the words you turn in. A word of warning here. If you are being paid by the published word, you retain the rights to all words edited out. Ask your editor to include a phrase in the contract stating that the rights to any words edited out of the body of work revert back to you immediately upon editing. It seems these days that some editors will edit out complete sections, only to use them as fillers later on. That's fine if you are paid for that work, but most of the time you will not be, and you'll be lucky even to find out that this has happened to you. This is a vague area in publishing contract law, so stand up for your words. If you're not paid for them, do not give the magazine a chance to use them in the future.
- *You pay them.* Yes, this does happen. Once your name makes the junk mail list for writers, you'll start to receive offers to write your poetry or story and, for a fee, have it published in an anthology. Sometimes a fee is not required, but buying the anthology is. If all you want is your byline in print, this could be your ticket. But work published in this manner will not count as a professional credit with editors.

When Will You Be Paid?

After you've established the amount you will be paid, the next big question is when. Advances in magazines are rare, so don't expect payment a week after your contract is signed. Magazines are pretty standard in their payment methods and there won't be much negotiating in this area, so it's best to know the magazine's policy before you sign the deal. Here are the usual methods of paying.

- *Paid on acceptance* is the best, and the most common, way to be paid among the large-circulation national magazines. Once your article is approved and accepted for publication, your check should go into the mail. Six weeks is an average wait to be paid on acceptance.
- *Paid on publication* is a popular way for magazines to issue pay, especially among smaller-circulation national magazines, locals, regionals, and the hobbies and trades. But because some magazines may not publish your piece for a year or more, you could find yourself waiting a long time.
- *Paid after publication* is not a common method, but it is used by many small-circulation magazines. The length of time is usually arbitrary, anywhere from six weeks to three months. Again, you may not be paid for months or even years.
- *Split pay*—half on acceptance, half on publication—is rare, but it does happen, especially for high-paying articles.

Belly Up

Magazines go out of business. Some cease publication forever; others are merely sold to another publisher with the intention of staying in business under a new editorial directive and often a whole new staff. Whatever the case, this can be a problem if you have a business transaction that hasn't been completed or a manuscript in their hopper when they shut their doors. There are several ways to deal with this situation, however.

First, if you submitted your manuscript on spec, have no contract, or haven't been paid for the project, the manuscript still belongs to you. Normally, when a magazine is sold or goes out of business the phone lines will remain open for a few weeks to handle inquiries from freelancers and others who have their work tied up with the company. Often the accounting department will remain behind even when the rest of the magazine has folded, so call and ask what's up concerning your work and any pay owed to you.

In the event that you have been paid or have signed a contract stipulating certain rights, the negotiations can be a little tougher. Those rights will transfer to the new owner, so call the new owner's representative—the managing editor or another high-level editor—and simply ask what will be happening with your article. Will it be published? When? Will payment arrangements stand according to the old contract? If there is no interest in your article, ask the magazine to reassign the rights to you. Make sure you get the reassignment in writing because this allows you to resell your work.

The bad news is that you may be stuck. It happens. You've been paid, but the piece isn't scheduled for publication or a clause in your contract allows the publisher to keep your work for an undefined period of time. However it happens, you do not have a work in print or one to which you have legal rights to resell, and sometimes there's not much you can do. One way to prevent this from happening is to ask for a publication date or issue designation in your contract or written agreement. (For example: Work to be published in the March 15 issue.) This may not necessarily be binding, but you can also ask for a clause stipulating how long the contract will be in force. (For example: Contract will be void two years from this date if the work has not been published.) These inclusions may help you retrieve something that might otherwise be lost.

Another thing. Because the new owner assumes the financial obligations of the magazine it is purchasing, it will be responsible for honoring your contract if you've worked out a deal to be paid on or after publication and you haven't been paid, even though your article was published by its previous owner. Be persistent about fighting for your money, because this particular battle can be tough. When you fail to get a response from one level of managemnt, go to the next one up and so on, until you make contact with someone who's willing to work with you.

And finally, when a magazine is bought by another publisher most articles already paid for will be published at some point unless they completely go against the editorial grain of the new company. Call and check it out. And if all else fails and your article gets hung up in magazine limbo, you still have your information to rewrite or query again.

Kill Fees

When you've established how much and when you will be paid, the next question to ask is if you will receive a kill fee. Most offers will come with a clause that your article must be accepted before payment is authorized. A sad fact is that some articles, even those under contract, will not be accepted. It may happen that your article just didn't turn out to be what the editor wanted, or the magazine took a new focus and your piece no longer fits. Whatever the case, some articles just don't make it, which is where the kill fee comes in. A kill fee is money paid to the writer for a completed article that was not accepted for publication. Kill fees come in a wide range, anywhere from 25 to 50 percent of the contract price. While some magazines offer them automatically, many do not. It's up to you to ask.

The Contract

Experienced magazine freelancers know that the skills required to write an article are considerably different from the skills required to negotiate its contract. Contracts and formal agreements vary from publisher to publisher. Most magazines offer them, but some will not. Some will bypass a contract by issuing a letter of intent.

How you want to handle this part of the negotiation depends on how badly you need the job, the paycheck, or the writing credit. If you are willing to risk your time and effort in producing an article without a contract and without a written agreement outlining what you and your editor have discussed concerning the article, go for it. Most publications will hold true to their word, but be prepared for the fact that some will not.

After you've had the initial discussion and have decided to write an article without a contract, outline the points of your conversation with your editor in a letter and send her a copy. Ask her to sign your letter and return a copy to you. Explain that it is just a document of clarification so both of you will have the same understanding about what it is you are writing and how the payment and other important issues will be handled. If your editor will not do this, most experienced freelancers will tell you to run away. But it's your choice.

A letter of intent or of assignment is still not a contract, but it is an acknowledgment from an editor that you are assigned to write a certain article for a certain amount of pay. It should include a deadline, the word count, and everything else pertinent to the assignment. Many editors use a letter of intent or assignment as a quick means to get right to the actual writing of the article, so normally when an editor goes to the trouble of spelling out the details in correspondence you can trust her to honor it.

The best situation is an assignment with a contract. In this case everything is spelled out in detail, all is legal, and everyone knows exactly what to expect. The details you have discussed with your editor, on all the important matters, will be included. There will also be issues you have never considered, however, that will have a bearing on your job as a magazine freelancer. Before we examine some of those issues, let's look at a few common questions always asked by freelancers who have not had the experience of negotiating a contract before.

1. *Do I need a lawyer or an agent?* Probably not. A lawyer might be able to help you wiggle out of a clause you do not like, but you can do the same, and when you consider the rate a lawyer charges against the amount you will make writing the article, can you really afford it? Besides, magazine editors are used to negotiating directly with writers. The same advice goes for hiring an agent. You don't need one to be published in magazines or to negotiate your magazine deals.

2. *What can I negotiate in the contract?* The pay and payment method, deadline, rights, word count, travel and phone expenses, kill fee, the editing process

(how many times you may be required to rewrite the piece), free copies on publication, and copies sent to contributors to your piece are the most common areas of negotiation open to a freelancer. When you get past the legal jargon required by the magazine's company attorneys, many of the actual writing and business details are very negotiable, but it's up to you to make the approach, because your editor will always stick to the standard contract.

3. *Realistically, what can I expect* in my negotiations? If the magazine offers one dollar per word, you won't get two dollars, but another few cents is reasonable. Jobs that will pay travel expenses usually go to the magazine's regular freelancers, but it never hurts to ask for them to be covered if you will be traveling any significant distance for your assignment. Telephone expenses are reasonable, however, and usually given. Deadlines can be adjusted by a few days, but asking for another month or six weeks is out of the question. Five free magazine copies is fine, but asking for 100 is ridiculous. In short, you can expect your editor to make some shifts in the magazine's standard offer, but you also have to expect that some will not be negotiable.

Every magazine has a different policy, and once you've worked for a particular one once or twice you'll know where you can ask for changes. Until then, use common sense and be reasonable. And, no matter how you negotiate your deal, get something in writing to back up the details of the agreement you have made with your editor. This is your job. Those details can make the difference when your phone bill for the assignment runs high or when you spend three weeks putting together an article your editor has no obligation to review or for which he is not bound to ante up a kill fee. They can also be invaluable if your editor leaves in the middle of your assignment and you find yourself working with someone new to you.

Consider Your Rights

The rights to your work are one of the most important parts of any sale you make to a magazine. Rights are your personal stamp of ownership and what you offer, or sell, to your publisher. Your rights protect you from having just anybody come along and use your work.

To new writers, rights are often also one of the most frightening concepts. Contract lawyers have written volumes on publishing rights, which is enough to scare anyone, but the definitions regarding rights are straightforward, especially for rights with magazines.

- First North American serial rights are the most common rights bought by magazines, and definitely the best rights for the writer to offer on a newly created work. Specifically, they grant the publisher the right to produce your article for the first time, and one time only. They allow you to retain all other rights to the piece. The reference to North American means that you are selling your first rights in the United States and Canada. The term *serial* refers to newspapers, magazines, and publications published on a daily, weekly, monthly, or otherwise regular basis. When you query or submit an article on speculation, note the rights you are offering so there will be no confusion for you or the editor making the purchase. Also, when you cash your check for the piece, make sure it contains no assignment of different rights noted as a condition for accepting payment. First North American serial rights are exclusive. They can be licensed to one publication only.
- First rights grants only the exclusive first publication of your work but does not specify where or how the material is to be published. Many of today's electronic markets prefer to negotiate first rights. To protect your other rights, you might want to consider

asking for a more specific definition of first rights, such as first electronic rights (discussed below). First rights are also used when you sell a piece internationally.

- One-time rights offer the nonexclusive sale of an article on a one-time basis. If you are attempting to sell your article to more than one publisher, you cannot offer an exclusive right, like first North American serial rights, so you offer one-time rights. Let your editor know that your article is a simultaneous submission if it is.

- Second rights or reprint rights are a clear statement that your work has been published before. They are used also in conjunction with portions of a book excerpted into a magazine. Second and reprint rights are not exclusive and you can offer them to as many publications as you wish, but always include a publishing history when you do. Also, when you offer these rights make sure you do so to a magazine that is not similar to or in direct competition with the magazine in which the article first appeared.

- All rights sell away your rights to the piece forever. This is a cheap way out for the magazine, especially if your article is something they will archive and reprint another time or print in a sister publication. Simply put, they won't have to pay you again, no matter how often they use your work. Because there is a resale market in hundreds of magazines, selling all rights will preclude you from finding other sales, inasmuch as you will no longer own the article. However, if you need the publication credit or if the pay is exceptional, you may have to let the rights go. The general advice from most seasoned writers is to be as stingy with your rights as possible and never give up anything you don't have to. In some cases, however, you might not have the choice you would prefer. In the case of selling all rights, you are selling only the article, not your right to reuse your information and sources and produce a similar, spinoff piece.

- Electronic rights, or e-rights, extend from online magazines (e-zines) and databases to CD-ROM magazines and publications to Web sites. This broad definition can be deadly to the writer because of its lack of specific distinctions. If you sell your e-rights to one form of electronic publisher, you may forfeit your right to resell it to another. For example, if you sell your e-rights to an electronic-format magazine you could even lose your legal right to post that work on your own Web site. So when you're selling your e-rights, be specific about what you're offering. Instead of offering the vague e-rights, try first Internet rights, one-time rights, or something that more clearly defines what you want to sell.

  Today many of the popular magazines have an online counterpart and are always on the hunt for articles. At the beginning of the electronic boom, magazines just assumed e-rights as part of first rights and published what they wanted without compensating the writer. Today, e-rights are a separate right, to be negotiated apart from any others. If a magazine wants your e-rights for their online counterpart, it may negotiate them as part of your original contract. There is now a growing financial boon from articles first published in print, then republished electronically by the same company. So sell this right carefully.

  On a discouraging note, services exist that resell articles, including electronic ones, splitting the profit between the publisher and the selling service. If you do not license your electronic rights carefully, you may run across your electronic article being priced at two dollars a sale, without a penny of it going to you.

- Subsidiary rights do not usually pertain to magazine writing, but just for your information they are rights covered in a book publication contract that include serial rights, audiotape, merchandising, foreign, translation, and a host of other rights that will never apply to magazine writing.

- Television, motion picture and dramatic rights are just what they say, which makes them rights most magazine writers will not encounter, especially in nonfiction writing. However, with a growing interest in reality-based television, if your story is explosive or you've found a great character to feature or are presenting something never before known to mankind, you might find yourself negotiating rights you never expected when you started the story. If you do get involved in subsidiary or television or motion picture and dramatic rights pertaining to magazine writing, consult an agent or a lawyer. Do not attempt to negotiate the contract yourself. Call your local bar association for the names of entertainment or contract lawyers in your area. To find an agent, browse your library for books—with up-to-date copyrights—about literary agents. Your library should also contain a current or at least recent issue of *Literary Marketplace (LMP)*. This volume lists agents.

  While there is no trade agency that officially represents literary agents, the Association of Authors' Representatives (AAR) does offer membership to agents who agree to abide by its code of professional ethics. For a list of AAR agencies, send your request (with a SASE having two first-class stamps) to the Association of Authors' Representatives, Third Floor, 10 Astor Place, New York, NY 10003, or find the information online at www.aar-online.org.
- Work for hire means you will be paid to do the writing but will have no legal rights to anything pertaining to the work, including the copyright, or even the right to expect a byline. If you enter into a work-for-hire agreement, you may even be prohibited—and possibly liable—under the copyright laws from producing a spinoff article based on research you conducted to write the original piece. Check your contract closely. Some publications consider all works submitted to be work for hire.

One last word on rights. The copyright laws exist to protect writers' creative works. Today copyright is implied. Once you commit your work to paper, you own it. As the law now stands, your copyright protects you for your lifetime plus a term of fifty years beyond. Titles, facts, and ideas cannot be copyrighted, however. For added protection you can file copyright papers legally, with the Library of Congress, for a fee, through the Copyright Office, Library of Congress, Washington DC 20559. If you don't want to go to this expense and you're still a little nervous about protecting your work, you can mark it Copyright (year) (your name) or © (year) (your name).

This if fine if you are distributing your work in a form that is not being considered for publication, such as a handout at a writer's conference, but since editors already know that your work is copyrighted, this notice runs the risk of offending them.

Entering into negotiations, picking apart the contract, and muddling your way through the maze of rights may all seem like daunting obstacles to the writing process. They can be if you let them. But to be a magazine writer who makes a living at it, you have to deal with all the angles of the business, including everything you've read in this chapter.

The first time you negotiate, you may not want to tackle a big list. Begin by trying for something like telephone expenses. Next time add a kill fee, then gradually move on to something else. Above all, use common sense. As you succeed in your negotiations, you will improve your skills as well as the financial benefits your work will produce. Although writing is your passion, it's also about making a living, so why sell yourself short financially when you don't have to? Editors will always make the lowest offer they can, so it's up to you to secure a better deal. And you will, with practice.

6
Getting Down to the Writing

Words in prose ought to express the intended meaning; if they attract attention to themselves, it is a fault; in the very best styles you read page after page without noticing the medium.
—William Hart Coleridge

Too MANY writers get hung up on the actual writing. Am I using the right words? Are my sentences too long? Too short? Should this be a new paragraph? Is my style too serious or too light? Where does this quote go?

The list of questions writers ask themselves as they approach the writing of a manuscript could fill pages, because they are about to make a public presentation for the first time. Their byline will be on display for everyone to see, their words heeded by readers. For the moment they will be the expert on the chosen topic, the person presenting a point of view to a few hundred, a few thousand, or as many as a few million readers. What they are about to write will suddenly transform itself from an idea in a few notes or a query into real substance.

As a magazine writer, you should be excited about preparing your manuscript. Your research is now completed, your experts are ready to go, your facts have been verified and proven suitable for your article, and your editor is convinced that your words belong in his magazine. Without question, what you have accomplished so far is the toughest part of the job. For someone who loves to write, however, the next step—the actual writing—should be the reward.

Basic, simple preparation works best. Brush up on grammar and sentence structure, then get ready to tackle page one.

Standard Manuscript Format

Every writer develops a personal manuscript preparation style. Unless a magazine requires a specific style of its own or an editor has a preference, the exact details of your presentation will not matter, as long as they contain the basic information laid out in a logical form. Some magazines do have manuscript preparation guidelines, however, so ask your editor about them before you start, or simply ask if there is any particular way your editor would like the manuscript prepared. If there is no preference, don't worry. The type of page-by-page preparation is not as important as many writing instructors would have you believe. Entire chapters have been devoted to how to construct the first page, and many lectures on the topic have perplexed more than one beginner. Even the question of where to put your personal information—in the upper left- or upper right-hand corner—has been the source of many debates. In truth, however, these aspects of manuscript preparation don't really matter. But here are some of the aspects that do matter.

1. Use plain white, 20-lb. bond paper. Never use colors.
2. Type in a plain, legible font. Avoid script and other fancy choices.
3. Letter-quality print (not dot matrix) is the only print accepted.
4. Always double-space. Editors need the extra room for editing notes.
5. Use one-inch margins on all sides but the top, where your margin will be approximately one and one-half inches, to leave room for a header. A header is your

page identifier above your text. This is also called a slug, or slugline.

6. Use proper page identification in your heading, including your last name, two or three key words that identify the title, and the page number.

7. Indent the paragraphs. Do not construct them in block form. Editors dislike having to insert indentations when they take a manuscript off a disk or scan the hard copy into their computer.

Titles

Many writers labor over what title to use. They may suggest one in the query, which is a good idea if you have an attention grabber, but the disheartening story of titles is that no matter how you may struggle to create something perfect, your title is only a working identification. What eventually sits atop your published article could be so different from what you wrote that you might not even recognize it.

Titles are quirky little things in which many writers invest too much time. Should they rhyme? Is alliteration appropriate in them? How many words should they contain?

Normally, when a topic comes to mind, a title soon follows. But the title is a place where editors like to express their creativity. In defense of the editor, he knows what will grab the attention of the magazine's readers, and will change your title to reflect that. Whatever the case, the odds that your title will make it to press are only fifty-fifty. Still, you need to know how to title your work, because your editor might after all deem yours a keeper.

Overall, titles should be catchy, simple, and on point.

An article about child safety in the kitchen could easily be titled "Staying Safe in the Kitchen" or "Kitchen Safety." Both are simple and sum up the content adequately, but do they catch your eye? Probably not. However, "Are You Risking Your Child's Life?" or "Protect Your Child Now!" will grab attention, because they express urgency and show that someone you love might be at risk. They are definitely catchy, short, clear indicators of what to expect from the article.

Consider using some of the following devices for your article titles:

- Rhyme: "A Claim to Fame"
- Alliteration: "Plums, Persimmons, and Pears: Three Recipes for Nature's Perfect Puddings"
- Challenge: "Do You Really Know What's in Your Multivitamins?"
- Statement: "Baby's First Christmas Can Be Memorable for Everyone"
- Shocker: "I Watched My Sister Die!"
- Drama: "Trapped in a Cave!"
- Statistic: "17 Teens Killed in Driving Accidents Every Day"
- Emotion: "Look over Your Shoulder—Are You Being Watched?"
- Clever Saying: "A Stitch in Time Saves More Than Nine"

Note that punctuation such as question marks, exclamation points, and colons are used in titles, but titles are never ended with a period.

Subheadings

Subheadings divide an article into sections. They help focus the reader's attention and allow the writer to change direction easily. Most articles are divided into subheadings. Grab a magazine and see for yourself.

On average, feature articles range from 1,500 to 2,500 words. The opening and closing should each contain about 5 to 10 percent of the total word count, leaving 80 to 90 percent of the entire word count devoted to the body of the article, with approximately 20 percent of the total word count included under each subheading. Here is how a 2,000-word article would be structured.

Opening = 200 words, leaving 1,600 words
for the article body
Subheading 1 = 400 words (20 percent)
Subheading 2 = 400 words (20 percent)
Subheading 3 = 400 words (20 percent)
Subheading 4 = 400 words (20 percent)
Closing = 200 words.
Total = 2,000 words

This is a pretty simple equation to use, but no one will penalize you if you vary it a bit. Maybe one of your subheadings has more information than can be crowded into 400 words, or your closing is only 50 words. That's okay. You can add or subtract words from the different sections, or even add or subtract a subheading if necessary. Also, if your sidebar word count figures into the overall word count, you can eliminate a subheading and make available that word count, or you can keep all your subheadings and subtract words from each section for the sidebar.

However you construct your article, make sure you include one of the following in each subheading:

- An expert's quote
- Information attributed to an expert
- An anecdote
- A combination of a quote, information, and anecdote

Base the entire theme of a subheading on what you have choosen. Here's an example.

Learning the Lessons

Eric, who was almost eleven months old on his first Christmas, was ready to celebrate and be the life of the party. "He knew about opening gifts by Christmas morning," says mom Eila. "He'd been practicing for days, on everything we put under the tree. He especially liked certain wrapping papers we used—the ones with cartoon characters, and the ones that were brightly colored." Bright wrapping paper, the most tempting of all gifts for the very youngest holiday enthusiast, is not usually a problem, but the contents of the box wrapped in that paper can be. Eila warns, "Make sure the packages you put under the tree won't harm your child if he opens one when you're not looking." Even the most diligent of parents can blink, though, which gives enough time for baby to grab that favorite eye-catching gift. Eila's advice? "Keep one or two unwrapped gifts under the tree to divert baby's attention from the wrapped ones."

As you saw, the subheading was set off to the left side ("flush left"), typed in boldface with upper and lowercase letters. When you write a subheading, always set it flush left, then underline it, use boldface, or write it in all caps. You need to choose a method that distinguishes it as a new section in your article, so pick one and only one style.

Oganizing the Details

As you were doing your research and conducting interviews, your article should have been slipping into its own logical order little by little. Articles usually do, long before you put anything on paper. Immersing yourself in your topic causes you to think about your article's objective, where you want to start and stop, and the points you want to make between beginning and end.

Organizing an article may seem a little difficult at first. You will have notes from several sources plus statistics, interviews, anecdotes, and a stack of odds and ends that seem to have a place in your article, but you're not quite sure where. By this point you're probably asking yourself how everything fits together and where it all goes.

Don't worry. Putting an article together is not as difficult as it seems, once you've found the key to getting organized.

Take a look at the following article organizer, then study the way the details of an article will slip right into it.

Article Organizer
Instructions:
To organize an article, complete the following outline, but don't worry if you can't come up with information to fill all the sections. What you need will come as you think about your article's objective. Make as many changes as you need, adding subheadings according to the word-count formula given earlier and using all the details necessary to say everything you want to say.
Work with your organizer in this order:
1. Complete the sections indicated by capital letters.
2. Complete the numbered sections.
3. Complete the sections indicated by lowercase letters.

A. Topic
B. Working title
C. Total word count
D. Article objective
E. Lead ideas (grabbers)

Subheading 1
(Repeat this section for such other subheadings as you need)
 F. Subheading title
G. Subheading objective
H. Subheading word count
    1. Details: fact/quote/information (repeat this section for all details you need)
        a. More information
        b. More information
I. Ideas for endings

Now let's see how this outline can look when filled out.

Article Organizer (Sample)
A. Topic: kitchen safety
B. Working title: "Are You Risking Your
   Child's Life?"
C. Total word count: 2,000
D. Article objective: To show commonplace
   kitchen safety hazards.
E. Lead ideas: This should be a grabber,
   something that catches the reader's attention immediately. It can be a relevant
   anecdote, a shocking statistic, or anything that will keep your reader from
   turning to another story. For example,
   20,000 home fires resulting in injury
   could be prevented each year, simply by
   paying closer attention to what's on the
   stove. Or, Sally turned away from the stove
   for just a second, but it took only that long
   for three-year-old Josh to pull a pot of
   boiling water down on himself.

Subheading 1
F. Subheading title: "Do You Really Know
   What's Happening in Your Kitchen?"
G. Subheading objective: Cite more kitchen
   hazards, with statistics from experts.
H. Subheading word count: 450
   1. Details: Every year, home safety mis-
      takes result in 7.3 million injuries,
      costing Americans more than $95 bil-
      lion, according to National Safety
      Council experts.
      a. There were 97,400 reported home
         cooking fires in the lastest year re-
         corded, "most of which could have

been prevented with a little caution," says one expert.

b. Most household fires start in the
kitchen. People walk away from the
stove or leave oven mitts or wooden
spoons near a lighted burner.

2. Details: "Fire detectors are a must,"
says a national Fire Protection Association expert. "They cut the risk of
dying in a home fire in half."

a. Place detectors on every level of
your home, and outside each sleeping area.

b. Check smoke detectors every month
by pushing their test buttons. Replace
detectors more than ten years old.

I. Ideas for endings: Conclude with something that leaves your reader with the feeling that the ten minutes just invested in
your work was worth the time. For example, hardware and department stores
will carry most of the items you need to
make your kitchen safer, so do your
checks, make your list, and go shopping.
Then know that with every safety precau-
tion you've taken you've reduced the risk
of accidental injury or death to someone
you love. For example, Sally's son Josh was
one of the lucky ones. His burns turned
out to be superficial and healed without
leaving scars. This was a hard-learned les-
son for Sally, but now her kitchen is so
childproof that even the most ingenious
child couldn't figure it out.

Keep adding more detail to each section until your article is practically written. At first, doing such methodical

organization will seem like a tedious process, but it allows you to build the structure of your article by laying a foundation, then adding to it. The organizer keeps you on track, focused on each section.

Eventually you may be able to skip this process—when you've written enough articles, their organization comes naturally. Until then, follow these steps and you'll be amazed at how close to a completed article you'll have once the outline is completed. And even when you get to the point where you can organize an article in your head, you may still want to use the outline occasionally when your article isn't coming together as easily as it seems it should.

Manuscript Pages

After you have organized the makeup of your article, the next step is preparing the actual manuscript, starting with page 1.

Magazine manuscripts do not require a cover page (a separate page containing the title, byline, word count, and author contact information), so page 1 must contain all this identification, including your name, address, phone number, fax number, e-mail address, and Social Security number, and the approximate word count. Place this information, single spaced, in either upper corner. Include the rights for sale if you are submitting a spec manuscript. For example:

Name
Address
Phone Number
Fax Number
E-mail Address
Social Security Number
Word Count
Rights

After you've placed your identifiers, space about one-third of the way down the page, then center your title, making sure it's enclosed in double quotation marks, not underlined (underlining indicates a book title). Type in upper- and lowercase. For example:

Name
Address
Phone Number
Fax Number
E-mail Address
Social Security Number
Word Count
Rights

(space)

"Title of Your Article"

Now drop down one single-spaced line from the title and write "by" in lowercase type, then move down one more single-spaced line and add your name, in upper- and lowercase. This might be considered a redundant step, since your name is at the top of the page already. But if you are using a pen name this is the place to insert it, indicating that it is a pen name. Just make sure your editor knows you are using a pen name so there will be no confusion when you submit the article. For example:

Name
Address
Phone Number
Fax Number
E-mail Address
Social Security Number
Word Count
Rights

(space)

"Title of Your Article"

by

JJ DeSpain, or JJ DeSpain (pen name)

Next move down three double-spaced lines, indent, and begin the article itself. Do not justifiy the text, but type flush left only. Justified text may look tidy, but this is a strict taboo in magazine writing. Many articles are scanned directly from the page into the editor's computer, instead of being typeset or retyped into another format, with some being taken directly off a disk. Either way, justification throws off the line spacing. Publications that justify in print will do it themselves, to fit their own page format.

Starting on page two and continuing every page thereafter, place a slugline at the top of the page, in either corner, and be consistent thereafter. After the slugline, move down to the normal starting line and
continue your manuscript. For example:

Last Name, Key Words, p. 2

Or another example:

Last Name/Key Words/p. 2

Sidebars will follow the logical paging progression at the end of the manuscript, indicated by the underlined word <u>Sidebar</u> at the top of the page, with the title of the sidebar directly below it, in quotation marks, as here:

Last Name, "Key Words," p.10

<u>Sidebar</u>

"Title of the Sidebar"

Every writer devises his or her own manuscript format, but as long as a manuscript is correct, neat, and in a basic variation of the examples just given, there will not be a problem. The differences in most acceptable styles are slight, but the information is consistent, and editors expect consistency.

Tending to the Details

When words that can be indicated by symbols are used, refrain from using the symbol and stick to the word. This includes percentages (50 percent) and degrees of temperature (99 degrees). Numbers have a different rule. One-digit numbers (five feet) must be spelled out, but two-digit numbers can be written in numeric form (40 yards). Addresses, phone numbers, and numbers in a list are written in numeric form too. Also, avoid abbreviations in favor of the full word, except for titles by which you address people, such as Dr., Mr., Ms., and so on.

Other important areas that bear watching are punctuation, spelling, grammar, and everything else that makes a manuscript stand out in its presentation.

- Use your spell checker if your word processor has one.
- Use a grammar checker, especially to find missed or incorrect punctuation.
- Be wary, however, of all grammatical suggestions offered in the grammar check programs. They are not always reliable sources of correct grammatical information. Instead, grab your grammar reference book off its shelf and use it.

Mistakes in grammar, spelling, and punctuation pop up in nearly all manuscripts, and editors expect that, so one or two won't hurt you. But a whole series of mistakes looks sloppy, leading to the assumption that if you are sloppy in the visual presentation of your manuscript you may also be sloppy in its content.

You are being paid to be a professional, and your work, no matter how brilliant its content, must look professional. With the amount of competition lining up, waiting to grab your job if you make a mistake, there can be no exceptions, so mind your details.

Transitions

The dictionary defines transition, as it relates to writing, as "a word, phrase, sentence, or group of sentences that relates a preceding topic with a succeeding one."

Transitions are another detail of good magazine writing that allow a story's progression to flow from sentence to sentence and paragraph to paragraph. Readers expect the flow to carry them along, to be led through an article without encountering skips in content or logic, which is what transitions do. They turn skips into a smooth flow and carry the reader—gently—from one idea to the next.

Transitions can be used for ideas going in the same direction, or to link ideas going in different directions. For example,

> If your fluid retention is coming from salt, increase your water consumption to flush the salt out of your body. If it's a result of hormones, there's not much you can do about it, but the good news about hormone swings is the *water will go away.*
>
> Speaking of *water* that *will go away,* checking your urine color is a good way to see if you're adequately hydrated.

The first paragraph is talking about having too much water in your body. Then the transitional phrase (in italics) leads into a discussion about finding out if you have enough water in your body.

Practice your transitions. Write a paragraph, then pick out a key word or phrase from the last sentence and use it to move into the next paragraph. The words or phrases do not have to be an exact match, just something close enough that your reader remembers he read that word or phrase ten seconds before.

Doing this creates a familiarity with what will follow through to the next idea, and familiarity is *comfortable*.

The *comfort* of reading is always a goal you should have in mind for your reader.

Writing Style

Style comes with experience, but it is also dictated by the magazine that is hiring you to write an article. Most magazines have a set editorial style, with reading the magazine being the only way to find out what it is. Knowing that style and writing in it may make the difference between being published in a specific magazine only one time or being asked back again and again.

In consumer magazines the style is normally casual and conversational. Imagine that you are talking to a friend, telephoning your mother, or explaining a concept to a child. Consumer writing is easy, the vocabulary not difficult. Slang is acceptable in limited amounts. So are occasional contractions, as long as you don't confuse *your* with *you're*. Profanity, though, is rarely acceptable, even in a direct quote from an expert, unless you receive prior approval from your editor.

Technical magazines require the jargon of the business. The writing in these venues is formal, written so as to instruct. There is rarely room for a conversational style here, and slang and contractions should be avoided. Trade magazines use a combination of the technical and the consumer style to convey a concept to a specific business. Because you are talking as one of them, a conversational style is acceptable, though in a version a bit more formalized than what you would employ in a consumer magazine.

At one writers' conference a participant complained that he had his own style, which he could not adapt to fit an editor's requirements. "Will it make a big difference if I don't conform?" he asked. If he doesn't conform to what the editor wants, that editor will find someone who will. And if he can't conform, he limits his writing opportunities and thus his paychecks. It's much easier to adapt your style to fit a magazine than to find a magazine to fit your style. A good writer is always adaptable.

The Subject

The first person pronoun is *I*, the second is *you*, and the third is *he, she,* or *they.* This basic concept that you learned back in grade school hasn't changed. In works of fiction, the third person is the most common form used, but the first person is also popular, especially in detective stories and gothic romances. The second person comes into play in nonfiction works that address the reader directly, usually to offer advice.

Magazines incorporate all three viewpoints in writing style, depending on the nature of the article. Articles about someone else are done in the third person. The first person is used when you write about yourself, and the second person is the vehicle by which to deliver advice. This book is written primarily in the second person, because its goal is to offer advice. There are passages in the third person thrown in along the way, but the only examples of the first person you will find are in the introduction and epilogue.

Should I Be PC?

Politically correct language is a difficult topic to address, because what is correct to some may not be to others. Also, the language changes, influenced by societal trends. What was accepted last year may have a whole new meaning this year.

The goal of politically correct language is not to offend. Years ago there was nothing wrong with calling someone a cripple, but the language changed to prefer *handicapped,* then *disabled.* Then, to reflect the person over the disability, the politically correct phrase became "person with a disability." Of course, there are other catch phrases used in describing people with disabilities, such as *physically challenged, differently abled,* and *handicapable.*

Generally there are no rules about PC writing except to be sensitive to the needs and feelings of the people about whom you are writing. If you are not sure about the correct term for referring to certain groups of people, call someone and ask. Almost any organization representing the group of people about whom you have a question can tell you what you need to know about referring to them as they would like.

Another area for PC debate is the proper use of *he* and *she*. When you are writing a generic article that includes both a male and a female audience, should you use *he/she* or *she or he?* You can use either, but they look awkward in print. Many writers are choosing instead to alternate the use of *he* and *she* between sections or chapters, as in this book. Making this change between sentences or paragraphs is too difficult to follow, but in an article use the division created by subheadings for the changes.

Minding Your Quotes

It should go without saying that when you use direct quotes in an article they should be written as closely to what was said as possible. Occasionally you may need to make adjustments for language or continuity, but never let these affect the content. If the content does not suit you, don't include it. Unfortunately, some journalists have a tendency to put words in their experts' mouths, but when this happens it defeats the purpose of having an expert in your article. You can take a few liberties with your quotes, such as breaking them into pieces you can use or sticking them into a section with a similar context, but never take them completely out of context, altering the original meaning. And when you do change the wording in a quote, read it back to the person you are quoting to make sure your changes are acceptable.

When you quote an expert, always write it up in the present tense. For example,"'Grandmothers' purses, full of pill bottles, are another source of poisoning danger for inquisitive children,' says pediatrician...."

Writing

Once your research is complete, your experts are lined up and ready to answer your questions, and you have found a market and committed yourself to a working title, created an article organizer, and decided how you will construct the first and subsequent pages, you are on your mark. After you are aware of the impact tiny details can have on an article, you are set but still not quite ready to go. Articles follow a logical progression from beginning to end. Once you understand that progression, you'll be ready to go.

The Article Lead

As you saw in the article organizer, the lead starts your story. It takes your objective for writing the article and combines it with something that will jump off the page and grab your reader's attention, compelling him to read on.

The goal of a good lead is straightforward: to get your story moving. A good lead sells your story at the very beginning, so your reader doesn't have to hunt to discover what the story is about. It's best to start with something that catches one's immediate attention: an anecdote, a statistic, an expert statement with a direct bearing on your article topic.

A good lead never begins a story with a subheading. Instead, it eases your reader into the article, captures his attention, and teases him with what's about to come. Begin with a one- or two-paragraph opening that will make a case for reading the rest of the article.

A good lead never takes a tabloid approach. Exaggerating a fact just to grab attention is not good journalism, even if it is a popular ploy. When you make a leading statement, be accurate, and be prepared to back it up with the facts.

A good lead avoids clichés and trite, overused expressions. Avoid leading with metaphors, too. For example: "In the evening of his life, Sam Smith took up flying airplanes." Instead, say "Sam Smith, at age 76, took up flying airplanes."

The Article Body

As you will recall from the article organizer, the body is the largest part of an article, comprised of the details you wish to present, all organized under separate subheadings. Several rules apply in writing the body copy.

First, be succinct. Consult your thesaurus for better word choices. And make your point, but do not repeat it unless your intent is to reemphasize it.

Again, know your grammar. In this regard also skip unnecessary adjectives, and avoid adverbs that are already implied in the verb. For example: "He ran quickly down the stairs." Instead, say "He ran down the stairs."

Follow a logical continuity. Start at the beginning and end at the end. Use your article organizer to help with this.

Don't plagiarize. Use proper citations when you borrow the work of others. This applies to paraphrasing, too. Do not commit libel, either. Libel is an untrue written statement that can damage a person's reputation.

The Article Ending

This part of the story closes your work, completes your objective, and lets your reader turn to the next story in the magazine with a sense of completion. Although only about 5 to 10 percent of a total article should be devoted to the ending, according to William Zinsser "the positive reason for ending well is not just to avoid ending badly but because a good last sentence—or paragraph—is a joy in itself. It has its own virtues, which give the reader a lift and which linger when the article is over." Consider the following approaches to endings:

- *Full-circle endings* loop back to the lead, drawing a conclusion that ties into the lead. In essence, they are transitions from the end back to the beginning.
- *Summary endings* are useful in list articles and how-to's, as well as in other teaching articles that set forth detailed facts. They pull out the most relevant points and restate them.

- *Quotation endings* leave you with the opinion of someone who can sum up what you've said. They agree with the overall viewpoint of the article, add one more touch of expert information or advice, or pose a question that challenges the reader to do more thinking on the subject.
- *Finish-the-story endings* complete a story that was started as part of the lead, and offer hope when the lead is a disturbing fact or statistic. The goal of finishing the story is to not leave the reader dangling.
- *Straight statement endings* allow the writer to use a few sentences to reiterate the point of the article and draw conclusions. In a sense, a straight statement can be a short editorial comment from the writer.
- *Advice endings,* like straight statements, allow the writer to end by giving his own advice on the subject.
- *Shocker endings* complete the story in a way that the reader did not expect. Maybe there is not a happy ending to the anecdote used in the lead, or perhaps the statistics are becoming more alarming. This ending leaves the reader with a disquieting feeling.

Editing Your Work

Some writers edit (revise a manuscript by making spelling, grammar, and content corrections, to prepare it for publication) as they write. They print out a page and perfect it, then print it out and perfect it again until it suits them. This process certainly produces a polished page, but it distracts from writing the pages that will follow, especially when the flow of your ideas does not stop at the bottom of each page. Also, there will be times, halfway through the article, when you will recall something that belongs on the first page. When you go back to add it, your hard-earned polish will go out the window and you will be faced with starting the editing process for that page all over again.

Since magazine articles are usually pretty short, most magazine writers pound out an entire article before editing it. If you get everything on paper before you start the editing process, you will find that the continuity of your article will be smoother. You will not have any great gaps in style or content, and the transitions from idea to idea will make more sense. Stop-and-edit writers are often faced with correcting style differences throughout the writing, as well as all the other things that require changing. They can have difficulty restarting the article from its stopping point, too, which wastes time.

Editing is one of the most important elements in producing a professional manuscript. If you think you can produce a finished piece in one draft that does not require more work, think again. No professional writer submits the first thing she writes.

Follow these tips for polishing your manuscript.

1. At the completion of your writing, use a spelling and grammar checker, but without relying on it too assiduously.
2. Set aside your work for at least 24 hours before you look at it again.
3. Read with a fresh eye. Look for spelling, punctuation, and grammatical errors, even though your word-processing program may have made corrections.
4. After you've spotted and corrected the mistakes, read for content and make any necessary changes.
5. Your third reading should be for word count. See more about this in the next section.
6. Now go back and repeat steps 1–5. Make corrections and changes as necessary, but avoid changing something only for the sake of change. Many writers become trapped in a never-ending editing cycle, never knowing when to quit. Generally, it's good to reread the changed section at least twice after changes have been made, but if you find yourself making changes that aren't really necessary, it's probably time to quit.
7. When you are satisfied that you've done everything you can, ask a trusted, and literate, friend to read and mark any mistakes. Also ask him to indicate areas where the meaning is unclear, but never ask

him to correct the content or style. These areas are solely your responsibility.

8. Make the necessary corrections and reread your manuscript.
9. At the end of your final reading, if something still bothers you go back and fix it. There's nothing worse than submitting a manuscript when you have a nagging feeling that you're sending out something that should have been changed.

Counting Your Words

Figuring word count in magazine writing is easy. You can either rely on your word processor to do the work or, since most articles are short, count the actual words yourself. Some writers prefer to take an average count, and while this method is used more in book-length works than in articles because an article's word count is often expected to be exact while a book's is not, it's still good to know.

1. Measure one inch of type lines (usually about three, if double-spaced), then count the words within that space.
2. Count the total inches of text lines on the page.
3. Multiply the words in the one-inch space by the total inches. For example, if your inch of text equals 35 words and your page of text measures 8 inches, multiply one by the other. Your average number of words per page is 280.
4. Multiply your average page word count by the total number of pages.

Magazine writers live and die by the word count, a practice that has existed since Charles Dickens became the first writer to be paid by the word. To understand why the word count is so important, you must first know that editors are apportioned a certain amount of space per article, into which only a certain number of words will fit. Unfortunately for magazine writers, the space allotments for words is decreasing, because the space for advertisements and photography is increasing. Advertising pays for the magazine, and good photography is one of the biggest customer draws, so words fall to the bottom of the list and the word count goes down.

With the tight constraints of a specific word count, you will often find yourself asking how you can write everything there is to say about a given topic in 2,000 words. The answer is you can't. Editors know that, and even though they may expect a 50,000-word book to be condensed into 2,000 words plus a couple of sidebars, they are realistic. They are also masters of pick and choose. As the writer, you must master this ordeal, too, picking and choosing the pertinent facts that are not widely known and the facts and concepts that can be easily understood by your readers, and getting rid of the rest.

Another thing you must understand before you begin writing is that because not everything will fit, some of the cuts you will be forced to make will hurt. This happens to every writer, each of whom has felt the pain of slashing away words he knows are the most brilliant writing he's ever produced just to make room for a fact that will have more impact on the article.

When you come to terms with the fact that the word count can be almost as important as what the words say, cutting becomes easier—not more pleasant, mind you—just easier.

What Gets the Ax?

The best advice to follow assumes that all writers, by the very fact of needing to express themselves, have too much to say, and that achieving the right word count is a matter of cutting, not adding. There are no hard-and-fast rules for what has to be to cut to meet your word count. Often it's just a matter of getting rid of superfluous words. Sometimes it turns into deleting entire sentences, paragraphs, or sections. Three general rules can help:

- Cut pet phrases, redundancies, and repetitions first.

- Cut phrases or sentences that make no difference to the objective of the piece second.
- Cut your opinion, if you are not writing an opinion piece, third.

When you've eliminated as much wordiness from these three areas as you can, it's time to find ways to condense your words.

1. Replace several words with a few words. For example, in "When you've eliminated as much wordiness from these three areas as you can, it's time to find ways to condense your remaining words," half the words can be eliminated by changing it to read "When you've eliminated your wordiness, find ways to condense the remaining words."
2. Use contractions when appropriate.
3. Rewrite long sentences. Break them up into smaller sentences, eliminating the words that joined them, such as *and, because,* and *or.*
4. Eliminate *that* as a conjunction to introduce a subordinate clause, such as "I think that she's leaving tonight." Instead, write "I think she's leaving tonight."

Cutting and condensing are both difficult tasks, leading some writers to strive to stay close to the required word count on the first writing, just to avoid being forced into dealing with cutting their words. The advantage to this is that it requires less editing. The disadvantage is that in the need to finish close to the count, important details might get left out of the article.

Other writers try to put down everything they want to say on paper before they give any thought to the word count. Certainly this can be a huge disadvantage if a writer is in the habit of turning out a 10,000-word manuscript for a 2,000-word assignment, because the cutting process will be overwhelming. The advantage, though, is that everything has been said that needs to be said. If the word count is exceeded by only a third or even a half, the cutting process will not be too difficult and you will be left with a nice margin for editing.

Editors need an editing margin too, which is why exceeding your word count by up to 10 percent in your final draft is usually acceptable.

When It's Ready to Go

Eventually you'll have to send your manuscript to your editor. By now you've worked and reworked it from every angle known to magazine writers, and your deadline is looming. The best advice is not to blow your deadline, even if your editor is willing to extend you a little more time. Blowing a deadline is unprofessional. Allow yourself plenty of time to finish your article and get it into the mail so it will arrive before its due date. Regular mail works, but priority mail is a good option too. You can also send your manuscript by certified mail, requesting a return receipt, so you'll have the peace of mind of knowing it arrived. A return receipt is also written proof that your article arrived on time.

When a deadline is absolute but you're a day or two away with a manuscript still in hand, invest a few dollars for overnight delivery.

Rewrites

Yes, rewrites do happen. Normally, your contract will obligate you to one or more rewrites. If it doesn't and your editor would like a rewrite, it's a good idea to agree to at least one, especially if you wish to maintain a good relationship with this editor.

Your editor will stipulate the exact rewrites he needs. It's best to get everything requested in writing. This agreement serves as your assignment sheet and proves that you have provided exactly what your editor wants.

Most editing changes are just a reshaping of the existing material, adding a different slant or taking away a part that the editor believes does not work. Sometimes a change in style or perspective is required, or maybe a different point of view from an expert is all that is needed. Often, editors will just call you to clarify one or two points, then do the rewriting themselves.

Don't be surprised, however, if you aren't asked for a rewrite at all. This happens when an editor is happy with your work.

Composing a manuscript, in spite of all the rules you've read here or learned elsewhere, is ultimately a matter of preference and style. William Zinsser says that good writing doesn't come naturally to anyone, and he's right. We may have a talent for writing, but talent doesn't always translate into good writing, which comes only with practice and hard work. According to Zinsser, "A clear sentence is no accident. Very few sentences come out right the first time, or even the third time. Remember this in moments of despair. If you find that writing is hard, it's because it *is* hard. It's one of the hardest things people do."

And one of the most gratifying.

7
Running Your Business

*Business is never so healthy as when, like a
chicken, it must do a certain amount of scratch-
ing for what it gets.*—Henry Ford

WHILE WRITING is your passion, when you write to make a
living your writing becomes a business, like it nor not. You
must operate it as such. Thinking in terms of profit and loss
in conjunction with one of the arts may be an alien notion,
because even when the arts are taught at the university level,
business courses are rarely a part of the curriculum. The
lack of business studies for people majoring in any of the
creative fields seems curious, considering it is usually the
goal of artists in all disciplines to work independently in their
art. Nevertheless, with or without a foundation in business
education, if you want to make a living as an artist your writing must be considered a business. Let us then consider what
is good for your business.

Finding the Right Time to Write

Finding time to write is one of the most important things you will need to do after you've made the firm commitment to write. That time must come without distractions, be consistent on a daily basis, and occur at a point in your day when you have the mental clarity to write best.

Once you have dedicated yourself to writing full-time, set aside a full-time block of hours in your day. Starting out, forty hours per week may be more than you need, but as you find success the need to increase your work time will adjust with that success. Sometimes this happens on a sporadic basis, but at other times it will be regular, depending on the workload you carry. Workloads in magazine writing are rarely consistent. Still, magazine writers are always hungry for work, so a dedicated forty-hour week may end up being the stopping place or, if you're lucky, the starting point.

Part-timers have a different situation. They are seeking work and struggling to juggle it with another job or the raising of a family. Full-timers don't have to juggle, unless they are putting in forty writing hours on top of another job, in which case the struggle becomes the same.

Think about where you find your time to write. Time is everywhere. It exists in small measures—ten minutes here, twenty there, or in larger blocks of an hour or two, or maybe even eight.

- During your twenty-minute drive to and from work, could you rattle off some article ideas into a tape recorder? Forty minutes daily to and from work over five days buys you a little more than three hours a week. Many writers would kill for an extra three hours.
- Could you set your alarm clock for an hour earlier in the morning? One hour a day times five days is five hours. Add that to the extra three during your driving

time and you have now picked up one full-time
writing day.
- Could you skip sleeping in on Saturdays or Sundays?
- Forfeit one television program every evening.
- Go to bed an hour later.
- Take a tape recorder on your morning run.
- Proofread on your lunch hour.

There are many different ways to find a little time in your
day, and even a little time compounded daily equals a part-
time career.

Many lecturers will tell you it's absolutely imperative to block
out several solid hours every day, and that is in fact the best way
to go, if those hours are available to you. There's nothing better
than closing your door to the world, then writing for two or three
uninterrupted hours. But honestly, who among part-time writers has that luxury, especially on a regular basis?

A well-known novelist knew she had to write, so every
night after she got home from work, cooked dinner, did the
dishes, helped her children with their homework, tucked them
in bed, spent quality time with her husband, and did a load of
laundry, she retreated to her desk under the basement steps
and wrote for an hour. Sometimes her writing day began at 11
P.M., but at others it started an hour or two later. The key to
her early writing success, when she was still a part-timer, was
consistency. She wrote every night before she went to bed.
Within three years, her first book was published and she had
become a full-time writer.

To succeed as a writer, it's not when you write or how
long, but that you write every day, without fail. You write when
you can, and use the spare minutes, because they do add up.
Make sure you're prepared for those moments when they do
happen, though. Always keep a pen and paper with you, or a
cassette recorder. If you have a project in the works, drag it
with you everywhere you go and hope a few minutes will open
up in which you can edit your work. Lug your stack of research

background reading along, too. You never know when you'll get a chance to read it.

Plan your writing time to be whenever you can. Schedule it into your activities, write it on your daily planner, and post it on the refrigerator so everyone is reminded, including yourself. Everyone can manage their time better, and if writing is really important to you, you will find a way to make better use of what's available to you. In short, a good writer, with a good writer's imagination, will create the time to write.

Avoiding Outside Distractions

Unfortunately, most people don't take writers seriously. Writing is often regarded as merely a hobby, a means of catharsis, a creative urge, but never a job. Most people do not respect a writer's writing time either, since it usually takes place at home. They don't consider that a quick phone call can break the train of thought, and it never dawns on them that dropping in for a few minutes can cost the writer a lot more than that in mental time.

Families themselves can be one of the biggest disrespectors of a writer's time. When you are at home, you are seen as being available to cook, clean, settle sibling disputes, run the kids to activities, deal with solicitors, and haul the dog to the vet. There are always expectations of you simply because you are at home. One magazine writer finally took up a full-time career when her children were all in school, and just as she was beginning to do well her father moved in. He knew she worked at home, but it never occurred to him that the game shows he watched, with the volume all the way up, disturbed her writing. It never occurred to him that when he asked her to join him for lunch every day he was interfering with her train of thought.

When you establish your business, set up ground rules to go with it. Let your friends and family know your work hours, and be emphatic that during those hours you are to be disturbed only in case of an emergency. Send flyers to let friends know your work hours, and be firm but gentle when you tell your mother to call back later. Don't answer the door when someone knocks. Use an answering machine to screen out unwanted calls.

One veteran magazine writer keeps a baseball hat handy. When it's on, she's at work. When it's off, she's fair game for anyone who can grab her attention. Her family abides by her "no interruption" rule. It's up to you to establish your own "no interruption" policy and teach it to your family and friends. Remember that it's your writing time that you are wasting when you allow outside distractions.

Setting Priorities

No one will disagree that family comes first, but exactly what parts of family life come first? Personal situations should top the list. There is probably no way to estimate how much time your family will need. For your daughter, ballet lessons could be an "I've got to have them or I'll die" situation. Little League might fall into the same category for your son. Your spouse certainly needs time, as do others, such as parents. These are priorities that you will have to deal with. But what about that slumber party your daughter wants to hold when you're on deadline? How can you prioritize that?

Everything in your life has a time and a place, and it's up to you to decide how that order falls when it deals with your writing time. Make a list for yourself. First draw a limit that works for you, then one that works for your family. Can you work a little extra the day before the slumber party, or could the party be postponed for a week? It's your life, and it may be a hectic one, but try organizing it into five categories to make it run just a little more smoothly. Make a list of your tasks for the day, then divide it into the following areas by priority.

1. What I absolutely must do.
2. What I should do.
3. What I'd like to do.

4. What I probably can't do.
5. What I absolutely can't do.

Make the list every day, every week, or every month, or whenever necessary to help you prioritize. When you commit yourself to these priorities, the distractions tend to disappear and the priorities to be accomplished.

Of course, if you live alone you don't have the problem of family distractions, but you will still have to contend with your friends in such a manner that, after the writing hours are over, they are still your friends. Fitting in time for friends and social life may call for applying the same five categories of prioritization.

Setting Aside Your Space

Having a regular workspace is important. You need a nook, cranny, or office to call your own when you take on magazine writing as a profession. If you don't stake out your territory, you'll be forever chasing down your scissors or favorite pen. Your kids will consider your computer their personal playstation. Your husband will dump his change and keys in your pencil drawer. Your wife will rearrange a stack of research notes that were in perfect, albeit sloppy, order. Your mother-in-law will abscond with your desk chair to use as a luggage holder.

You need your own space to establish your identity as a writer, including to those with whom you live. Establishing space engenders respect. It tells everyone you are serious about what you are doing. When you take yourself seriously by setting aside the space you need, you increase the likelihood that others will take you seriously. But you have to use that space appropriately once you create it, or no one will take you, or it, seriously. A politician in the Midwest, newly elected to office, set up his home office. He bought a nice desk and a filing cabinet, then built some shelves. It was a great office, but he didn't use it, and soon the door was opened only once or twice a month. After the first year went by, his wife stuck the cat litter box in the office because it was an out-of-the-way, never-used room.

The amount of space you set aside for yourself is not as important as the fact that it exists. Chances are you may not have room available for a separate office. But ask yourself:

- Do you have a corner in your bedroom or the utility room that would accommodate one of those put-it-together-yourself computer organizer desks? For a little privacy in your corner, buy or make a screen to separate you from the rest of the room.
- What about an enclosed back porch, or the basement?
- Maybe part of the garage?
- That space under the stairs?
- The guest bathroom no one ever uses?
- A closet? Don't laugh; many writers do set up in closets. One best-selling romance writer turned a coat closet into her office. Her husband hung a droplight, and she used an upside-down cardboard box for a desk and sat cross-legged on the floor.

Be creative with your space. It doesn't have to be large, but it does have to be efficient. Your chair should be comfortable, your desk adequate for your equipment. Keep your basic references within reach, and reserve a small area just to stack your stuff—the books you're reading for your current project, or the magazines you intend to read when you have a few minutes. Having a file cabinet is nice, too. In fact, if you don't have room for one, consider purchasing a couple of two-drawer file cabinets and placing a door or some sort of sturdy top across them to suffice as a desk–file-cabinet unit. Buy some brackets and boards, then add some shelves to the wall space surrounding you.

Your office might not make the cover of a home-decorating magazine, but if it is functional and efficient, and conducive to your writing, that's really all you need.

The best of all possible writing situations is a dedicated office, not one that coexists as a guest room or has any function other than being your office. An extra bedroom is good, or a large walk-in closet works. A room built to serve as an office is wonderful.

In all situations where you do have your own room, you can arrange your writing equipment to suit you and not have to make do with a laundry basket serving as a filing cabinet or a droplight as a desk lamp. Be judicious about your space, though. Start out with what you need, not what you want, unless you have an overabundance of room. And don't begin by cluttering your space; let the clutter come later.

One of the best investments you can add to your office space, no matter how large or small, is a fireproof safe or fireproof storage box. Naturally, as a writer you will be backing up your documents regularly on disk. Store those backups in a fireproof container so that in case of an accident, if your computer is destroyed, that's all you'll lose.

Don't get too bogged down setting up your office, because this is not a difficult process. Office supply stores have everything you need, from desks to filing cabinets. There are many companies that build custom-designed offices, including desks and shelving, to fit your existing space. This can be a blessing if your room is limited and you want to utilize what you have to its fullest potential, but it can be costly, too. So if cost is a huge consideration, don't rule out secondhand stores, garage sales, and antiques malls.

One other note on your workspace. Make sure everyone knows that what's in your space is not for general use. It is not to be borrowed or used when you are not around. If you can afford a computer for your writing use only, do it. If not, apportion computer time, with the clear understanding that none of your files are to be touched and nothing in your writing space is to be bothered. This goes with respecting your space and respecting you as a writer.

Going to Work

One of the great advantages of writing is that you don't have to go far to go to work. There is no commuting time, no traffic jams. You don't have to pay to park, and you definitely don't have to budget for gas money. Still, you do have to prepare yourself to work, even if you're going only as far as the corner of your bedroom. When you go to work, as with any job there are certain choices to make in your work day.

Dress

Okay, so you can knock out an article in your underwear and no one will know. Sounds good, and some writers do it. Of course, you can also go to the Barbara Cartland extreme and dress in a flowing, sequined nighttime formal as you take on your day's work.

Dress is a personal choice. One of the advantages of working at home is that you don't need a special work wardrobe. A general rule of thumb for most writers is to dress as you would to spend a day around the house. When you treat your writing as a job and approach it as such, down to your manner of dress, you are showing a degree of respect for your work and for yourself as a writer. But after all is said and done, if you still produce your best writing in your boxers, do it.

Breaks

As you are establishing a work pattern, factor in breaks and a lunch hour, just as you would on any other job. Writing is a tough business. It drains you mentally, which leads to physical tiredness. You'll find that you are just as tired after eight hours of writing as you would be from any other job. So you'll need breaks to keep your mind fresh, refocus your concentration, and stay alert. You'll need them too to prevent eyestrain and aching muscles. When you put in a full eight hours, never go for more than two before you take a few minutes to stretch your muscles, give your eyes a rest, and get your mind off the project. Go take a big drink of water, eat a high-energy snack, or whip through a few exercises.

Allow yourself at least half an hour for lunch. Have it with your spouse, invite a friend to join you at a nearby restaurant, or grab a sandwich and take a long walk. Just make sure you get away from your work, because most writers know that after a couple of hours the thought processes often begin to go soft.

Writer's Block

It happens. You sit down to write and nothing transpires. The more you concentrate on what you need to accomplish, the harder it is to transfer an idea to paper. Writer's block is a catchall term for any number of reasons that prevent a writer from writing. Outside distraction, lack of interest in the topic, poor concentration, and health problems are just a few. You could be tired or experiencing eyestrain. Your mind could be on a sick friend. A medication could be making you drowsy. You might be experiencing a reaction to a high pollen count.

Writer's block can be overcome simply by writing. When you have a problem getting your thoughts transferred to paper, force yourself to write anyway. You'll probably have to go back and do some heavy editing, or even delete something you wrote when you were facing resistance, but keep up the practice of writing even when you think you can't. Often just the act of writing lessens the resistance, blocks out the distractions, and restores interest and focus.

Maybe you're a writer who doesn't block or has never had a day when you couldn't produce something, yet suddenly the effort to write is formidable. You can't think, can't create, can't find a new idea. Even the computer keys are presenting an obstacle. This could be a sign of a physical problem. You know when you have the flu or a cold, and you can expect some down time until you recover. But maybe you are experiencing symptoms that you are not aware of. There are medical conditions that can affect your ability to write when they are under control: Anemia robs your brain of oxygen, and diabetes and low blood sugar cause loss of concentration.

When difficulty in writing is persistent and not normal for your writing routine, check with your doctor.

Keeping Records

If you claim your business for tax purposes, retain every scrap of paper that will prove you are doing business as a writer. Keep a mileage ledger, and by all means hang on to those rejections. They prove that you are trying to make a living. Because the IRS is leery of writing as a profession, these rejections could be important if you are audited and have to prove your claims. Also, keep sales receipts for every purchase you make in conjunction with your writing, whether for postage stamps or paper clips. File your papers in an orderly fashion, and create a balance sheet to verify your expenses at the end of every month. It can be simple: a spreadsheet or a simple log covering the basics—what, when, how much, and why. Or you can purchase computer programs for running small businesses.

For beginners, a basic system of your own creation, similar to the ones that follow, can work just fine. It will satisfy the IRS, especially when you can produce the documentation such as receipts to back up your claims. If you do not have a receipt for an expenditure, such as for photocopies or postage from a machine, record that no receipt was available, and include the reason. Be very careful about keeping items for business and personal use separate.

Business Purchases

Date	Item Purchased	Cost	Receipt?	Business Use

A mileage log can be just as simple. Record only your mileage for business use.

Business Mileage

Date	Destination/Reason for Trip	Odometer Beginning & End	Total Miles

Here are a few other tips about records.

1. Establish a separate checking account to use only for your writing business. This will make record keeping easier and help you keep track of your expenses. Write checks whenever you can, and avoid using cash.
2. Check the current tax laws before you make any decisions about taking your business as a deduction, or investigate what expenses incurred in your business can be deducted. The tax laws change every year, so call your nearest IRS office and request the most up-to-date information.
3. If you attempt to do your own taxes, consider using one of the many good tax programs available in most computer stores. When your work starts rolling in and you receive dozens of statements at the end of the year from each of the magazines that employed you, preparing taxes can get tough.
4. Subscribe to a trade magazine such as *Writer's Digest*. It is usually filled with tax tips for writers every year around tax time.
5. Check your library for books on the business and legalities of writing.

Supplementing Your Freelance Income

Most freelancers will tell you it's tough to make a full-time living, even when you are doing full-time writing. Unlike the freelancer who is embarrassed to admit that he moonlights writing obituaries, most magazine freelancers will tell you that they take on odd jobs to help make ends meet. That's part of the writing life, especially for beginners who want to make a success of working at home before their career begins to catch on.

Numerous writing opportunities exist outside the freelance magazine market. Just look around at the volume of printed material you see every day—brochures, newspapers, newsletters—the list is endless. For every page or paragraph of copy in print, a writer is making money.

You can earn that money too when you start making your services available. You might want to consider some of the following jobs:

- Newspaper stringer.
- Political writing. Call your favorite candidate and ask if a position is available. Politicians are often interested in good speech, brochure, and op-ed writers.
- Writing letters or constructing résumés.
- Typing and editing college research papers.
- Teaching word processing.
- Starting a business that offers a variety of writing services. Create a brochure or flyer listing your services and send it to small businesses in your area. Post it at universities, then be brave and hand deliver a few to larger companies. Have some inexpensive business cards printed, too.
- Write a greeting card. In fact, write dozens of greeting cards. One will not pay much, but several together can produce a good income. Write to Greeting Card Association, 1030 15th Street NW, Suite 870, Washington, DC 20005 for more information. Also consult *Writer's Market* for companies that accept freelance greeting card submissions, as well as novelty gift submissions such as mugs, t-shirts, and bumper stickers.

Exhaust every writing possibility you can think of. Be creative. If it's going to be in print, someone has to write it, and that someone could be you.

Running your own business can be a headache if you let it, but there are easy ways to circumvent the difficult problems. Use common sense. Don't immerse yourself in unimportant detail. Create a simple business plan that fits what you are doing: if you are writing only one article a month, you certainly don't need a comprehensive business structure that would suit the likes of megaselling novelist Stephen King. Look for library resources that can help you. Invest in software programs for business and taxes. Above all, don't let the business end of your work take over your writing. You are a writer first.

8
The Finer Points of Success

*I believe the true road to preeminent success in
any line is to make yourself master of that line.*
 —Andrew Carnegie

WHEN YOU'RE a writer, making yourself a master of your line means
going beyond the ordinary writing efforts to seek out the finer
points of your craft. It's not enough that you be a good writer or
have your topics well researched and your queries on point. It's
not even enough for your manuscripts to be polished and professional, and to meet your deadlines without fail. To achieve the
road to preeminent success, mastery is found in the nuances, in
the places other magazine writers overlook.

Moving Forward

Forward is the only way to move if you want your magazine
career to grow. To move forward means to keep working on your
writing skills: to select one aspect of your writing and strengthen
it, or try writing a type of article you've never attempted before.
It means spending more time in the library searching for new

resources, rereading your grammar book, and creating a new and more impressive letterhead for your queries.

Moving forward is about making things happen in your career instead of just sitting back and waiting for them to happen. It's a daily process that advances you beyond where you were yesterday while you're keeping an eye on where you'd like to be tomorrow. You are ready for a new challenge and always on the hunt for something that is not yet part of your career. You jump on every opportunity that arises, or create new opportunities when what you want or need isn't happening.

The only thing that will move your career forward is you. Your writing may be great, but if you don't show it to someone you're not moving forward. Your knowledge of query techniques may surpass that of most writers, but it you don't use it you're not moving forward.

To move forward, perhaps it's time to examine several approaches. Take an honest look at where you're going, and compare it to where you'd like it to go. Are you on the right track, or have you changed course? Would you like to get back to your original track, or is where you're headed okay? Can you add another track to your career path, or is there one that should be taken away? Do you have a long-range goal for your career? Finally, do you have a strategy to get you where you want to go?

Now take a clear-eyed look at your talent and assess its weaknesses and strengths. Is your writing really as good as you'd hoped it would be? Are you working on the areas you know need improvement? Is your writing stacking up against that of other writers in your subject area? Have you been thinking about trying something new or dropping something old?

Writing Associations and Conferences

Writing is a lonely business. There's no one in the office but you. No one to talk to, and no one to listen. Still, even the most die-hard hermit of a writer likes to shed the solitary existence from time to time and connect with other die-hard writing hermits. For some, the peer connection happens in a writing critique group, but to be honest, once your career is going strong and you are spending forty or more hours a week writing to meet deadlines, you may start to move away from your group. Your interests will change and your time commitments to writing may increase to the point that the hour or two you spend with your group would be better spent on your career. Many published writers feel that because they are being critiqued regularly by the people whose opinions count the most—their editors—peer critiquing is no longer necessary.

Whatever the case for moving away from your writing group, it does happen as many writers begin to achieve success. The result is that they find themselves isolated from any writing connection.

There are dozens of associations in North America that not only provide a connection to other writers but offer professional services, encouragement, news of the industry, and benefits ranging from insurance coverage to discounted office supplies. Many of the large national writing associations are also influential in pushing their specialty in the writing industry forward in behind-the-scenes negotiations dealing with issues such as contracts, pay, and current standards. The American Society of Journalists and Authors regularly challenges contracts unfavorable to nonfiction writers, while the Society of Professional Journalists takes on political issues that affect a journalist's right to access information. The Romance Writers of America have transformed a small writing genre into a force that captures the largest percentage of paperback book sales.

Organizations exist for almost every writing specialty, from medical writing to science, and most of these national organizations produce a newsletter or magazine to keep their members in touch with the entire writing industry as well as what's going on in their particular area of interest. They often hold conferences, on both the regional and national levels, and there's no better place to connect with other writers than at a writing conference.

Check these resources for listings of writing associations: *National Trade and Professional Associations of the United States, Writer's Market,* and *Literary Marketplace* (LMP).

Promoting Yourself

One of the perks of magazine writing is that it's an anonymous job. Readers don't attach the same significance to a magazine by-line that they do to the credit on a best-selling book, even when the writer of the magazine article may have more readers per month than the book author will ever have in a year.

The book author, however, has an instrument called a publicist by which readers will come to know the writer's name and when his next release is due. A book publicist's job is to promote the writer and his work. This is done primarily to establish the writer's reputation and credibility, which in turn sells books.

Magazine writers rarely have publicists, however, because one article in a magazine volume will not influence the sale of that magazine one way or another. So there is nothing to be gained—for the magazine, that is—by promoting a magazine writer. There is everything to be gained by having the magazine writer promote herself, though. Self-promotion creates visibility, and visibility leads to job offers.

Some writers send press releases or updates to editors and others in their writing circles. This step could be viewed as too aggressive and egotistical. However, after you've completed an assignment, a thank-you letter to your editor for that assignment, with mention of several of your latest projects, is in order. Make sure you include several suggestions for future articles, and always end with a sentence such as "I look forward to working with you again in the near future." If nothing else, such a letter tells your editor you are still a working writer and you'll be back.

Another way to promote yourself is in your queries. As mentioned in Chapter 4, list your credits. Pick your very best work and send clips from those.

Inevitably, once you are working regularly for one magazine, one of its rivals will want you, because what's good for their competitor is also good for them. So after you've completed a few assignments for one magazine, target its nearest competitor and show what you've been doing for their rival.

Promote yourself everywhere you go, including at the writing seminars you attend. This is called networking, where you affiliate with a group of people with the same or similar writing interests. Networking becomes a "you show me yours and I'll show you mine" situation, except that when you show yours you never know what the results will be. Someone who's watching could know someone who needs what you're showing.

Always carry clips of your best work to show or distribute, and be liberal about handing out your business cards. Shake every hand you can find, and talk about your successes. A magazine writer with a nice but struggling career found her writing affiliation through a university-sponsored writing workshop. Each year as her successes mounted she talked about them to other attendees, sharing her knowledge of what it takes to succeed in magazines. Pretty soon she was giving mini-lectures in the hallways and restrooms. Other writers knocked on her hotel room door at odd hours of the night, and she was surrounded by an entourage at meals. One of the other participants, an aspiring publicist, listened to the writer, then promoted her services to the director of the workshop. The writer eventually returned to the workshop as a guest speaker. After that she moved into a nice side career teaching at writing conferences.

Don't overlook the media as a means of promoting yourself. If one of your self-help articles makes it into a popular magazine, call your local radio and television stations to tell them you are available to be interviewed about that article. Send a brief statement about where your article appeared, your bio, and a copy of your article to the city editor of your newspaper in case he needs a human-interest piece. Ask for mention of your article in the column that highlights the accomplishments of local residents.

Self-promotion is nothing more than taking advantage of every situation in which you can talk about yourself and your work. Every writer who is good at self-promotion knows to follow a few basic guidelines:

1. Keep a current résumé handy at all times. Trifold brochure stock, available for purchase at most office supply stores, can turn an ordinary résumé into a professional-looking brochure.

2. Have a good-quality photograph taken. One word of caution here. Professional photographers own the rights to the pictures they take, even when the likeness on that picture is of you. When you have a professional picture taken, you may need to secure permission to use it each time you do. Find out before you make the commitment. If you have a friend who's a photographer, preavail upon that friendship.

   Note that glossy photos do not reproduce well. You may need to have your photo reproduced in halftone (black and white) so it can be copied into your brochure or résumé.

3. Assemble a publicity kit consisting of your photo, brochure or résumé, business card, and several complete examples of your work. A two-pocket folder will hold this information nicely.

4. Whenever you make a public appearance, have your clip file with you. These do not have to be original clips; originals are often hard to come by, and you risk losing them when you take them anywhere. A portfolio of copies of your best articles works just as well. In these clips, attach a photocopy of the magazine's front cover. This showy touch helps people looking at your clips identify with the magazine.

Teaching

Sharing what you know with writers who are striving to carve out a career like yours is one of the great ways of giving back while you're moving forward. Besides instructing others on points they need to advance their writing, teaching helps you put what you know into perspective. It forces you to think about what you are doing when you write, analyze the steps you take for granted each time you turn on your computer, and put a logical order on the process you call your job. In other words, teaching heightens your awareness of your writing and serves as a reminder of what you are doing right—and wrong.

When you teach, if you listen to what you are saying you will improve your craft. The reason is that you teach empirically in that teaching is based on practical experience rather than theory. As you instruct others from your own experience, your subject matter becomes a personal story. You will always present the best you have to offer when what you offer is based on your own experience. In many cases, what you teach may even turn out better than what you apply to your own writing. The reminder about sending in queries in 9 × 12 envelopes, instead of folding them into a legal size, seemed good when you learned it, and you did practice it, but years ago. However, it's something that has gone by the wayside over the course of your career. When you instruct your students in proper procedures, you will remember that tip and probably put it back into your own routine.

Writing is one of the few areas where professional credits, not academic accomplishments, matter. The same goes for teaching writing.

- Opportunities exist at all writing conferences.
- Universities seek professional writers to teach continuing education classes.
- Some corporations hire writers to instruct employees in writing techniques.
- Many libraries and bookstores offer writing workshops.

To snag a teaching job, you must first promote yourself. Check the writing magazines and *Literary Marketplace* for upcoming conferences. Select the ones that list writing topics similar to what you might teach, then send your publicity kit, with a letter indicating your interest in participating as a lecturer. If you have no experience, offer your services for free as a way to get started. Fees will come later, when you have gained teaching experience.

If you attend a conference that you particularly like, offer your teaching services for the next conference. Make yourself known to the conference directors; afterward, follow up with a letter and a request to be considered as a lecturer. Ask a fellow writing buddy to send along a recommendation too, or approach a conference director if you have established a good relationship. When brochures advertising a writing conference come in the mail—and they will once your name makes it into writing circles—send an inquiry about participating as a speaker. Or grab two or three friends who are enjoying success similar to yours and establish your own conference.

Teaching gives you a credential that your writing does not, but it will not happen until you have established yourself in your writing field. It is probably not a goal for a first- or second-year writer, but perhaps in your third year you could start by teaching a course on what it's like to be a struggling beginner in the magazine industry, or on ways to parlay success.

Reinventing Your Career

One thing leads to another, and what you are writing today may be light-years away from what you'll be writing next year. Sometimes your career moves in a certain direction by choice, but often it drifts in a way that seems to fit.

Eventually you may want to return to your original writing choice, if you didn't get to start there. Or you may wish to forsake your original choice for something else. Perhaps teaching appeals to you, or you'd like to try your hand at writing mystery novels. Maybe you'd just like to turn your general business articles into hard-core financial or investment advice.

Writing careers are reinvented as opportunities present themselves. One magazine writer specializing in consumer articles hadn't contemplated writing nonfiction books until her editor recommended her to a book publisher who was looking for a contributor for a consumer advice book. That recommendation reinvented her career.

Careers are also reinvented because a writer is bored or stalled, or just needs new challenges. Many are nonetheless reinvented as a means of moving to another level with different opportunities, including that of better pay. At some point you will probably reinvent or expand your writing career in new directions. This happens to most writers. No matter how it comes about, there is some basic advice to heed.

1. *Don't burn your bridges.* With the uncertainty of writing jobs, you may need to cross back over.
2. *Keep a goal in mind* and work toward it, but never overlook an opportunity that presents itself out of the blue. Maybe you have no idea how to write a screenplay, but if the offer comes up, you can certainly find a collaborator who would be thrilled to help you.
3. *Use your work as stepping stones,* taking the small steps first. If you want to be a health writer but have no prior experience writing health articles, start with health fillers. Then work your way up to single-page articles and finally go for the features.

Getting Out of a Writing Rut

Some of the best lessons of success—the finest points of your success—were defined at the beginning of your writing career. Back then you had the basic rules in front of you, and you stuck close to them. They created security and a continuous line along which your career advanced. But magazine careers are risky because of the factors you have read about in this book, and one day you may have found that to avoid risk you allowed yourself to fall into a rut. You may have stuck with an editor you don't particularly like, because he will buy almost everything you write. Or you are writing for less than you're worth, because to ask for more money is to give your editor a chance to shop around for someone else. You may stay in a writing area that no longer interests you because you are achieving some success in it and switching could mean a cut in pay or the loss of regular work.

All these and other reasons aside, you're still stuck in a rut. Unfortunately, it could turn into a huge reflection of the writing you are producing, because a writer's attitude and emotions do show in her writing.

Take a look at your early writing, then compare it to what you're doing right now. Did the early writing have a sharp edge to it while your current work is rounded at the corners? Is your early work full of enthusiasm, unlike your current writing, which is run of the mill? If you can answer yes, perhaps it's time to look back to your beginnings and figure out what you did then that got you to where you are now.

Go back to Chapter 1 here and reacquaint yourself with why you wanted to write for magazines. Then move on to Chapter 2 and think about why you chose the article category you did, or why you decided to be a niche writer. Reinventing your career is nothing to fear. Writers do it every day. They stay where they are, or move in different directions, or both. Part of the reason any successful writer is a success is the love of a good challenge, and reinventing your career is always a challenge. A multimillion-dollar fiction writer had a career any writer would want, but after years of what he considered to be the same old thing he was in a rut. His solution was to write a few nonfiction articles about computers, an area where he had at one time been considered an expert. Unfortunately, his first few articles were rejected. The challenge mounted, and he worked even harder at getting an article published. It took nearly two years, but now computer articles are a successful sideline and his greatest challenge, because he receives rejections like any other magazine writer. His fiction career still runs smoothly, bringing in millions of dollars, but his magazine career is the challenge that keeps him out of his rut.

The finest point in any writer's career is defined by that person's ability to find the writer inside, even when that individual is trying desperately to lose herself. Writers get lost every day, give in to defeat, believe that their stack of rejections really means that they cannot write. They put their writing on a back burner with the intention of saving it for another day. They choose their obstacles carefully. But a writer who truly has the passion and the guts to write will do whatever it takes to fulfill that dream.

Epilogue
The Write Attitude

*No act falls fruitless; none can tell how vast its
powers may be;
nor what results, enfolded dwell within it silently.*
—George Edward Bulwer-Lytton

As a former attendee and now a lecturer at writing seminars throughout the country, one of the questions most frequently asked of me is, "What if the editor wants one thing and I don't agree? Do I have to do it?" The answer is no, you don't. You never have to do what an editor wants. But then you won't get the job, either. And you probably won't get the next job, or the one after that, because until you have learned to grit your teeth and say, "I can do that," you won't be doing *that* very often.

I start my lectures to nonfiction magazine writers by having them grit their teeth, snarl a little, and grind out those all-important words, "I can do that."

"I can do that." To get the job and to keep an editor coming back for more, these are the most important words you will utter.

"I can do that" are the words that will bring in your paychecks.

"I can do that." The truest test of a magazine writer's character lies in an ability to subordinate what she wants to the demands of the editors and the magazine.

One thing you have to remember when you take up magazine writing is that the editorial goals of the magazine always come before the personal goals of the writer. There are no exceptions, but that's okay. Good work is produced every day by magazine writers who have learned that they really "can do that."

Magazine freelancing is tough, and don't let anybody tell you otherwise. So little depends on your overall efforts, so much on the whims and trends of the magazine industry as a whole. But magazine freelancing is a great job, and don't let anybody tell you it isn't. There are limitless opportunities to write about new ideas and meet new people. And the opportunities to be published are much more abundant in magazines than for any other kind of writing.

"I can do that." The reality is that there are more constraints placed on magazine writers than on writers in almost all other writing disciplines, largely because magazine writers are reaching larger audiences than any other writers. They are also exerting an influence that would probably boggle their own minds if they gave it much thought. Think about the influence of the magazines in your life. Did your mother swear by what she read in *Better Homes & Gardens*? How many meals did she prepare straight from their recipe pages? Could you wait to read your next edition of *Boys' Life*? Did you just die when *Seventeen* ran a feature on your all-time favorite teenage idol? Did your grandfather talk about delivering the *Saturday Evening Post* when he was a boy?

One of the most influential magazines in my life was the *Weekly Reader*, passed out in school. I felt important having a magazine of my very own, starting in first grade. Years later, when I was approached by *Current Health 2*, a magazine for teens produced by the same company that published *Weekly Reader*, I didn't hesitate to say yes. The pay offered was much lower than what I normally get and the deadline was almost impossible in my busy schedule, but the chance to be a part of something that had so much influence in my life was an opportunity I couldn't pass up. So after the demands were laid out by the editor, even though I knew I could spend the same amount of time and effort producing an article that would pay ten times more, I smiled and said, "I can do that."

And I'm glad I did. I sincerely hope your career in magazines produces the same wonderful opportunities for you.

Glossary of Magazine Terms

All rights   Selling all aspects of ownership to the piece, forever.

anecdote   A short account, usually personal or biographical, about something of interest.

angle/spin   The perspective from which you write a story; the point of view: the best way to present your idea. *See also* peg.

anthology   A collection of similar works by different authors.

article   A nonfiction composition that is an independent unit in a magazine or newspaper.

article outline   *See* proposal.

assignment   A story that has been requested by an editor; the word count, topic, focus, fee, and kill fee are established as part of the process of making the assignment.

as told to   Stories told by someone who has had an unusual or particularly interesting life experience, to someone who can record that experience.

B&W   Photographs developed in black and white.

bimonthly   Every two months.

bio   A brief statement about the author at the beginning or end of an article. It usually contains the author's name, place of residence, and a few key writing credits.

biweekly   Every two weeks.

business-size envelope   The standard envelope used in business correspondence, also called a #10 or legal size.

byline   The author's name on the published work.

Caption   A brief description that accompanies a photograph.

check contract   A statement printed on the back of a paycheck indicating the rights that are being purchased to the story.

clean copy   A manuscript that is clean in appearance and free of serious errors.

clips   Examples, usually photocopied, of your published work.

column inch   A measurement by which some magazines pay their writers; one measured inch of a typeset column.

consumer/service journalism   A category of articles that tells the reader something he should know to make his life better or performs a service to the reader.

consumer magazine   A publication covering a wide range of topics aimed at readers with a general interest.

continuing education   Classes offered by universities for the purposes of helping people stay current in their fields or providing information in areas of interest.

contributor copy   An intact copy of the publication in which the writer's work appears.

copyediting   Editing a manuscript for spelling, grammar, punctuation, and printing style only. *See also* editing.

correspondent   Part-time freelance contributors from a specific geographic location who submit occasional material to a magazine. The newspaper equivalent is called a **stringer** (q.v.).

cover letter   A one-page letter accompanying a manuscript, with a brief description of the manuscript.

cover page   A separate manuscript page containing title, byline, word count, and author contact information; not usually required on a magazine article manuscript.

Deadline   The established date when an article is due to the editor.

department   Short items that appear under the same heading every month.

Editing   To prepare for publication; to shape a manuscript for content and form. *See also* copyediting.

editor   The person vested with the responsibility for generating and revising a work for publication. See Chapter 3, "Know Your Editors," for a description of editor categories.

electronic submission Submitting a work remotely by modem or by mail on a hard disk.

el-hi Elementary to high school audience.

e-mail Electronic mail, generated on a computer and sent and received on a computer.

expository writing Sets forth facts; takes current topics, news items, and newly discovered information and turns them into salable articles that explore all perspectives of an issue.

e-zine A magazine published in the electronic format.

Facsimile transmission (fax) An electronic form of communication used to transmit documents over telephone lines.

fact checking Checking the facts of an article for accuracy.

feature In newspapers, an article that is not hard news. In magazines, a lead article.

filler A short nonfiction item to fill out a newspaper or magazine page.

fiction A work based on the imagination.

first North American serial rights Permission granted to a publisher to produce an article for the first time and one time only, which allows you to retain all other rights to the piece.

freelance (free-lance) From the Middle Ages, referring to an independent or mercenary soldier who was free to offer his services—symbolized by his lance—for sale to any employer. Today a freelancer often sells his writing services to a number of different employers.

Galley A typeset version of the manuscript, without paging, often sent to the writer for revisions.

ghostwriter   A writer who is paid to write a work for another person's signature.

glossy   A black-and-white photo with a shiny surface.

grabber   *See* hook.

guideline   An instruction sheet defining exactly what a magazine wants in an article: it will tell what areas of the magazine are open to freelancers and what types of articles the magazine requires.

Hard copy   A printout of a manuscript on paper.

header margin   The space above the text into which the slugline goes. *See also* slugline.

how-to   An article that teaches how to do something.

hook   The opening of a story, or story section, that captures a reader's attention, also called a grabber.

human interest   A true-life article reporting an unusual life story or dramatic event from the writer's perspective.

Illustration   A drawing, as opposed to a photograph.

indirect quote   A statement that is paraphrased instead of quoted. The rephrased statement is not enclosed in quotation marks, but the person who made it does get credit.

Internet   The worldwide computer network offering access to a variety of resources.

International reply coupon (IRC)   A coupon purchased from a post office that can be redeemed for return postage from a foreign country.

interview article   An article written on the basis of a conversation between a writer and the one from whom information was sought.

Jargon   The specialized language of a profession or group.

journal   A personal journal is a record of one's thoughts, feelings, and observations. In magazine form, a journal is a professional collection of works and studies written for members of a specific profession.

Kill fee   Money paid for a completed article that was not accepted for publication.

Lead time   The time between the date when an article is accepted and the date when it is published.

letter-quality submission   Print that looks typewritten, usually from a letter-quality dot matrix, bubble jet, or laser computer printer.

libel   Making false accusations or statements in print that can damage a reputation.

list   A no-nonsense compilation of facts, similar to a how-to article (q.v.), except that the how-to will cover the details of the theme, whereas the list will highlight helpful tips and the bare facts.

literary fiction   Considered to be intelligent, nonformulaic, experimental, and serious; not usually found in mainstream magazines.

Manuscript   The typed version of an article, abbreviated ms. (manuscript) or mss. (manuscripts).

masthead   The page listing the editorial staff, usually found near the beginning of a magazine.

model release   A statement from a model to a photographer granting the photographer permission to use a photo.

multiple sales   Selling an article to more than one market at a time, by means of "one-time rights" (q.v.).

multiple submission   *See* simultaneous submission.

Niche   One writing area.

nonfiction   Writing based on fact, not imagination.

On spec (speculation)   Sending an article not assigned by an editor, one that the writer is speculating will sell.

one-shot feature   In syndicating, selling a one-time article as opposed to a series.

one-time freelancers   Freelancers who publish once only in a magazine and do not have an ongoing relationship with that publication or an editor there.

one-time rights   Selling the nonexclusive rights for one publishing only of a work.

op ed (opposite the editorial page)   A piece written as a response to current editorials and topical subjects.

Page rate   The pay per printed page.

parallel submission   Developing and submitting several articles from one area of research.

paraphrase   To restate a passage or text in other words, often to clarify the meaning. Spoken remarks that are paraphrased are attributed to the source.

pays on acceptance   Pays when the article is accepted.

pays on publication   Pays when the article is published.

peg   The angle from which a nonfiction writer develops an article. *See also* angle/spin.

pen name (pseudonym, nom de plume)   The use of a name other than the writer's legal name on the writer's works.

periodical   A publication issued at regular intervals.

personal essay   An essay written from the writer's perspective about an aspect of his life.

photo feature   An article in which the photos are emphasized over the written text.

plagiarism   Using the work of another writer and claiming it for oneself.

point of view (POV)   The way a writer views or considers something.

potboiler   A writing project designed to bring in money quickly, with a minimum of time and effort.

proofreading   Reading for and correcting of typographical errors.

primary research   The original facts that come directly from the source.

proposal   A detailed description of an article you are offering; also called an article outline.

Query   A letter proposing an article you would like to write.

Regular freelancer   A freelance writer who receives work from an editor on a regular basis.

Reporting time   The time it takes an editor to respond to a writer's query or on-spec manuscript.

Reprint rights (second rights)   The nonexclusive rights to reprint an article for publication, meaning that you can offer it for reprint publication as many times as you like.

Round-up article   A piece composed of comments and interviews from several people (often celebrities) on one topic.

SASE   Self-addressed, stamped envelope.

secondary research   Research coming from something another journalist has written.

semimonthly   Twice a month.

semiweekly   Twice a week.

serial   Newspapers, magazines, and publications issued on a daily, weekly, monthly, or regular basis.

service/consumer journalism   This category tells the reader something he should know to make his life better.

shorties   Similar to **fillers** (q.v.), but in the department category. Shorties range from 50 to 300 words and are grouped together with three or four other shorties on a similar topic, all appearing on one page under a common heading such as health tips, beauty facts, or household hints.

sidebar   A boxed section in an article that offers highlights, resources, or information that parallels the article but does not fit into the body of it.

simultaneous submission   Submitting an article for consideration to more than one market; also called multiple submission.

slant   The style of an article that will fit the preferences of the magazine in which it will be published.

slicks   Magazines produced on slick, shiny paper; usually used in conjunction with the top-selling national magazines.

slides   Photos taken in positive color slide format; also called transparencies.

slugline (slug)   Information included at the top of each page: the writer's name plus a few key words describing the article's title and a page number.

slushpile   A collection of unsolicited materials received by an editor.

spin/angle The perspective from which a freelancer writes a story; the point of view: the best way to present an idea.

stringer A part-time, freelance contributor from a specific geographic location who submits occasional material to a newspaper. The equivalent contributor in most magazines is called a **correspondent** (q.v.).

style The manner in which an article is written.

subheadings Explanatory headlines that divide an article into sections.

subsidiary rights Do not usually pertain to magazine writing; they are rights covered in a book publication contract that include serial rights, audiotape, merchandising, foreign, translation, and so on.

Tabloid A publication in a particular newspaper format.

target audience The groups of readers to which a magazine aims its editorial focus.

tearsheet The actual page from the published article, used as a clip.

trade magazine A periodical that covers the news of a specific trade or industry.

transparencies *See* slides.

Work for hire Work that is generated and owned by the publisher and hired out to a writer. The writer owns no rights to the work and, often, no rights to the research either.

References

Anderson, Ian E., ed. *Editor & Publisher International.* New York: BPI Communications, 1998.

Bjørner, Susanne. *Newspapers Online,* 2nd ed. Needham Heights, Mass.: BiblioData, 1993.

Edwards, Tyrone, ed. *The New Dictionary of Thought.* Standard Book, 1964.

Fulton, Len, ed. *The International Directory of Little Magazines & Small Presses.* Paradise, Calif.: Dustbooks, 1997. Annual.

Holm, Kristen C., ed. *Writer's Market.* Cincinnati: Writer's Digest Books, 1999. Annual.

Literary Marketplace. New Providence, N.J.: R. R. Bowker, 1999. Annual.

Mallegg, Kristin B., ed. *Gale Directory of Publications and Broadcast Media.* Detroit: Gale Research, 1998. Annual.

Polking, Kirk, ed. *Writing A to Z.* Cincinnati: Writer's Digest Books, 1990.

Reader's Guide to Periodical Literature. New York: H. W. Wilson, 1999. Annual.

Russell, John J., ed. *National Trade and Professional Associations of the United States.* Washington, D.C.: Columbia Books, 1996. Annual.

Strunk, William, Jr., and White, E. B. *The Elements of Style,* 3rd ed. Needham Heights, Mass.: Allyn & Bacon, 1979.

Waithe, Deborah, ed. *The National Directory of Magazines.* New York: Oxbridge Communications, 1992.

Webster's New World Dictionary of the American Language, College Edition. Cleveland and New York: World, 1962.

Wood, Clement, ed. *The Complete Rhyming Dictionary.* New York, N.Y.: Doubleday, 1991.

Zinsser, William. *On Writing Well: An Informal Guide to Writing Nonfiction,* 5th ed. New York: HarperPerennial, 1994.

Associations Cited

American Society of Journalists and Authors (ASJA): 1501 Broadway, Suite 302, New York, NY 10036.

Romance Writers of America (RWA): 3707 FM 1960 West, Suite 555, Houston, TX 77068.

Society of Professional Journalists (SPJ): 16 S. Jackson St., Greencastle, IN 46135.

Magazines Cited

Better Homes & Gardens: 1716 Locust St., Des Moines, IA 50309.

Boys' Life: PO Box 152079, Irving, TX 75015.

Byline: PO Box 130596, Edmond, OK 73013.

Cosmopolitan: 224 W. 57th St., New York, NY 10019.

Current Health 2: 900 Skokie Blvd., Northbrook, IL 60062.

Family Circle: 376 Lexington Ave., New York, NY 10017.

Humpty Dumpty: PO Box 567, Indianapolis, IN 46206.

Jack and Jill: PO Box 567, Indianapolis, IN 46206.

Saturday Evening Post: 1100 Waterway Blvd., Indianapolis, IN 46202.

Seventeen: 850 Third Ave., New York, NY 10022.

The Writer: 120 Boylston St., Boston, MA 02116.

Writer's Digest: 1507 Dana Ave., Cincinnati, OH 45207.

Index